A
Brilliant
Life

A Brilliant Life

RACHELLE UNREICH

HARPER

NEW YORK · LONDON · TORONTO · SYDNEY

HARPER

Originally published in Australia and New Zealand in 2023 by Hachette Australia.

A BRILLIANT LIFE. Copyright © 2023 by Rachelle Unreich. All rights reserved. Printed in the United States of America. No part of this book may be used or reproduced in any manner whatsoever without written permission except in the case of brief quotations embodied in critical articles and reviews. For information, address HarperCollins Publishers, 195 Broadway, New York, NY 10007.

HarperCollins books may be purchased for educational, business, or sales promotional use. For information, please email the Special Markets Department at SPsales@harpercollins.com.

FIRST US EDITION

Library of Congress Cataloging-in-Publication Data:

Names: Unreich, Rachelle, 1966- author.
Title: A brilliant life : my mother's inspiring true story of surviving the Holocaust / Rachelle Unreich.
Description: First US edition. | New York : HarperCollins, 2023. | Includes bibliographical references.
Identifiers: LCCN 2023029093 | ISBN 9780063328754 (trade paperback) | ISBN 9780063328730 (ebook)
Subjects: LCSH: Unreich, Mira, 1927-2017. | Blumenstock family. | Holocaust survivors--Czechoslovakia--Biography. | Unreich, Mira, 1927-2017--Family. | Unreich, Rachelle, 1966- | Children of Holocaust survivors. | Spišská Stará Ves (Slovakia)--Biography. | Melbourne (Vic.)--Biography.
Classification: LCC DS135.C97 U578 2023 | DDC 940.53/18092--dc23/eng/20230621
LC record available at https://lccn.loc.gov/2023029093

23 24 25 26 27 LBC 5 4 3 2 1

For my father Emanuel 'Manny' Unreich (1916-2005),
the first champion of my writing,
I carry your name with the utmost pride and love

Preface

Melbourne, 2016

My mother has always told her stories perfectly. When her grandchildren were little, they would long to stay overnight at her house – in part for the nightly ritual of hot chocolate and the heavy European bedding that wrapped them up in a bubble of goose down until they succumbed to sleep, but mostly for the magical way she could tell a story. She would give different voices to each character, her expressions veering as wildly as the plots. She was a master of improvisation – if the small listener cried out that they wanted an enchanted kettle, for example, she would quickly introduce one – and each tale finished on a triumphant note.

But today, as she tells me the story of my birth, there are no funny voices, no extraneous details. She is matter-of-fact, deliberate, the way she is whenever she talks about the past. It goes like this ... It was 1966, and my mother, Mira, was seven months pregnant. It was her fourth pregnancy, and while the others were easy, this one was not. Her feet were impossibly swollen, and she had recently become sick with a cold. She decided to ease herself into a hot bath to relieve her aches; when she got out, her waters broke. My panicked father drove her to the hospital, where it was discovered that she had a high fever. Her obstetrician was summoned and, since it was the middle of the night, he rushed in with his pyjamas on underneath his clothes. He delivered me at four in the morning, and I was so tiny and sickly that I was not even weighed, but instead whisked away to be placed in a humidicrib. When my mother recounts this to me, she simply recites a series of facts, and her voice does not falter when the story takes a turn, when it is clear that her newborn was frighteningly unwell.

'You were very sick. You had a complete blood transfusion, and you had something wrong with your lungs. The doctor said, "I don't want to be optimistic. It could be that she will not make it, so don't count on her."'

I lean in closely, trying to establish how my mother reacted. With shock? Fear? It is hard to tell. She talks about her husband, instead. 'Your father started to cry; he was already so emotional. I said, "Don't worry, she's going to make it, I know she will!"

'And two days later, the doctor came and said, "I've got to take her out of the humidicrib." We asked why and he replied, "She is banging on the glass. She is going to break it; we can't afford it!"'

I believe that this happened. I was born two months premature and I did, apparently, bang on the contraption's sides. Throughout my life, my mother has told me this story many times, exactly this way. The facts never changed. Even the words themselves are fixed, the same phrases reiterated.

The tale of my birth symbolises something for each of us. To my mother, Mira, it is about my inner strength and potential. Even when my body was tiny, she knew I was never weak. She also wants me to know that something powerful lies within me, and has always been there in spite of what science and history and statistics otherwise claimed. She never wants me to doubt it. It is a quality she recognises, because she possesses it too.

For me, this is a story about my mother's faith. While my father was in tears, half-expecting me to die, my mother refused to fold this into her thinking. Even though the doctor warned her not to become too attached to me, she knew he would be proved wrong. I can't imagine Mira was fearful; even for a minute. It is in her character to completely banish such negative thoughts from her mind.

I am hearing this account once again because I have decided to interview my mother while she is still able to speak easily. She is eighty-nine and cancer has been worming its way through her body for several years. She senses the days are running out, I can tell.

It is my last chance to learn some of the details of her life, which has known both beauty and brutality. But more importantly, it is an opportunity to discover the origins of her deep belief. I am curious about the unwavering steadiness of her faith. As her pace to the end quickens, she is not scared that before her is an unknowable void; she does not entertain the notion that she might soon be stepping off into nothingness. That is because her experience of the universe is one where the inexplicable happens, and where the thread of magic skips across the edges of the darkest fabric. How can my mother be so certain of what lies ahead for her?

Slowly, slowly, I will find out.

Part One

Prologue

End of September, 1942
Częstochowa, Poland

Boarding the freight train, they were told to keep moving even when each car was full. Even when it was dozens of people past full. The threat came early: if one person went missing, ten would be shot in their place. Jews were shot all the time; those who had been too slow to embark had been shot. Their captors would make good on this particular promise.

They all stood upright, limb against limb, pressing into each other. Before long, the air became stiff, filled with human stench. The only slip of light was through a window high above. In this box – could you call it a carriage? It was a coffin – some of them had started collapsing, dead. In the beginning, the passengers had been shrill and anxious, asking each other, 'Where are we going?' Now there was little talking.

David Milgrom thought of himself as a man of faith; as such, he had to have faith in himself. He could not afford to focus on his maddening thirst, these phantom fingernails in his throat. Instead, he began working away on a small hole in the wall, using a nail he'd found on the ground. But when the others saw what he was doing, they implored him to desist, some using their fists for emphasis. *Don't do it! Don't do it for the sake of us all.*

He regretted having listened to that chorus as soon as they came to their final destination. When the doors of the train opened, he was immediately set upon by men with clubs and sticks, who shouted at him furiously: 'Get out!' The crowd surged forward in a rush, many getting trampled in the process. And then this place.

Although there were the jarring features of an ordinary train station around him – a clock, timetables, signs and a ticket office – they receded against the awful, disorientating scene that he faced. It was indescribable chaos. Children were crying, mothers were screaming out for the children they had lost in the confusion, and all the time there were men waving sticks around, together with large dogs barking and the ugly yelling of armed SS officers and Ukrainian guards: '*Schnell, schnell!*' Quickly, quickly.

Orders came at him like bullets that he had no time to dodge. 'Take off your shoes and tie them together! If you do not do so in sixty seconds, you will be shot!' He obeyed, only to discover that sharp stones were scattered across the path, tearing bloody cuts into his bare feet. 'Put your shoes in that pile! Put your coat here! Put all your money there!' The bags held close for days on the train journey lay discarded in mounds which grew larger and larger, swelling quickly. Bulging, misshapen monsters.

The new arrivals were soon divided into two. To the left – the elderly, infirm and orphaned. David was shunted to the right, with the remainder.

'Take off all your clothes!'

Could that be correct?

They were forced to strip naked, males and females both. When the women were led to a different section, he watched them covering their breasts with their arms, as if their modesty was the worst thing they could lose.

His group was ordered to collect all the clothing, documents and valuables that had just been discarded, placing the money in open suitcases, the clothes onto a high stack. As they did so, running back and forth down a pathway, they were flanked by the same guards who had hit them as they alighted the train, beating them viciously once more. David was shocked when he realised that these men were Jewish, like him. There was no point asking them why they were doing this, because he could see why: Ukrainian guards stood at their rear, threatening to kill them if they weren't sufficiently brutal. They were *Kapos*, prisoners assigned by the SS to supervise work details. Their instinct was to survive; David had the same instinct.

And yet these *Kapos* were still his brethren, so David tried firing questions at them as he ran. 'What will happen to us? How do I get out of here?'

They ignored him, avoiding looking into his face, until finally one *Kapo* answered him in a whisper: 'Try to get dressed.' And so the next time David went to throw clothes onto the pile, he grabbed some of the items instead, shoving his legs into pants, pulling on a waistcoat. From another pile – now grown as tall as a building – he collected a pair of shoes. There were thousands of men running; he prayed in the mayhem that he would not be spotted.

No longer naked, he had only one choice if he wanted to be inconspicuous: stepping in line with the *Kapos*, pretending to be one of them. In a single sweep of movement, he picked up a thick tree branch that had been lying on the ground and began waving it wildly about. He tried not to think about connecting with the scalp of a neighbour, the arm of a friend. '*Szybciej!*' he yelled at the naked prisoners in Polish as their feet lifted the earth from the ground, small pebbles flying, dust everywhere. '*Faster!*'

In the distance, he could hear the screams of the women, a solid wall of sound. It went on for several minutes, maybe. And then it stopped, and there was silence. Later, he tried to see where they had gone. All that remained were the dresses they had shed, ugly now, like a pile of butterfly wings that had been ripped from the insect. *What is really happening here?* he wondered. *How can I escape from this place?*

* * *

For four days, he acted the part of a *Kapo*, the same scenario repeating over and over, a nightmare playing on a loop. Jews would arrive at the station as he had, many thousands in a day – only now he was one of those yelling. Once, he saw a crooked old man hobble off the train, and was ordered to take him to the *Lazarett*, or 'the hospital'. This turned out to be a massive open pit, a fire burning below, the cavity filling fast. David gently helped the old man undress, folding his clothes by the side of the pit, even though he knew the man would have no use for them anymore.

By now he had discovered what happened to the people who had disembarked with him. Those on the left, the weak, who could not fight back? Like the old man, they were shot and thrown into a burning pit. As for the others: the women were forced to have their hair shorn, and each group was made to run naked along a long path to a chamber. Perhaps they felt a prickle of relief when they reached the brick building at the end and saw a Magen David – a Star of David, the symbol of the Jewish people – at the front. A curtain hung over the entrance, and in Hebrew, the words were inscribed upon it: THIS IS THE GATE TO THE LORD. THE RIGHTEOUS ENTER HERE. Inside, cramped as they were – they had to raise their arms to fit in – some might have let their guard down a little more when they saw the shower heads and taps fixed to the walls. They were here to wash themselves, that was all.

When everyone was inside, the doors were sealed. Then carbon monoxide exhaust was pumped in. The path that the prisoners had just run down? The Germans called it *Himmelfahrtstraße,* or 'the Road to Heaven'. Within thirty minutes of their 'shower' starting, everybody was usually dead, although not instantly and not always. Treblinka II was never designed to be a work or 'transit' camp, as the SS had called it. It was a killing centre. Even the train station features that the prisoners had seen on arrival were fake, a wicked trick: they had been placed there when the death camp was built so that those newcomers, earmarked for extermination, did not panic at the outset.

The scent of death was literally never far; there were prisoners whose job it was to move the corpses from the gas chambers and into the mass graves, and it was easy to detect who they were when they crossed over to David's side of the camp: a cadaverous smell permeated their skin, and the stench emanating from them was impossible to ignore. For much of the day, David's task was to sort out the piles of clothing so they could be shipped to Germany. There were often heartbreaking remnants among the abandoned items, each of which had their own story. Sewing kits, teddy bears, flasks of cod-liver oil, photos, prayer books, Kiddush cups. Those working alongside him were ordered to look for money and valuables hidden within the clothes and hand it over to the SS. Here they revealed a glimmer of their rebellion: sometimes, they would put precious things into their own pockets. Occasionally they burned the banknotes so the Germans couldn't have them.

At every chance, David talked about running away, urging others to join him. He was met with incredulity. Escape? Unthinkable. The men were monitored constantly, counted four times daily. At night, a light from the guard tower shone into the window of their barracks; any movement would be detected. The camp was well fortified. And even if one evaded the constant watch of the SS, then what? Capture was inevitable.

But David did not see another option: when he asked these men how long they had been at Treblinka, the answer was five days, maybe ten – none of them had been there for longer than three weeks. He began devising a plan, enlisting two other young men to join him. It was futile to try to implement it in daylight, when any transgression would be easily spotted. The night would provide some cover, and perhaps a blessing; in the Torah, the day and all its promise begins with the sun's setting and not its morning rise.

And so, instead of returning to their barracks at the day's end, the three men stayed with the huge bundles of clothes that were already outside, rolled and stacked for removal the following day. Earlier, when tying them together, David had devised a hiding spot; in the centre of two of the rolls he and the others had left a hole large enough for a person to squeeze inside. His partners concealed themselves in one, he in the other. In their pockets, they had some valuables they had found in the clothing. Each man also carried a large knife, stolen from the kitchen; if they were caught, they would not die without trying to defend themselves.

From inside his fabric cocoon, David watched the Ukrainian guard who patrolled the area with a torch, and timed the intervals when the light was no longer shining in their direction. Lying in the shadows, he counted the minutes the way a man counts the ticks of his pulse, training all his focus on those beats. They had half an hour, he estimated.

When the sky turned inky black, the men left their hideout and took cover behind the thick wall of smoke – David called it the 'smoke of prayers' in his head – which was continually rising from a pit of burning bodies. At just after one in the morning, the trio crawled towards the enormous barriers that kept them imprisoned.

The first internal fence had prickly pine and juniper branches woven into its gaps, partly to serve as camouflage from the outside world. When the men realised it had soft soil at its base, they began to dig a hole underneath it, using their knives as shovels.

Next, they encountered a barbed-wire fence, and the earth was hard. They had no choice but to climb over it, and over another one after that. Scaling them was exhausting work, although careful planning saved them from grave injuries; they had each pilfered an extra layer of clothing to protect themselves, including gloves.

Finally outside the camp, in the middle of a dense forest, they faced a dilemma. One man wanted to head towards the nearest village, even though a curfew meant that any movement in the streets would be detected. David and the other man favoured a different approach; they would hold tight, lying on the ground without moving until it was light. That first fellow left alone. An hour later, the barking of guard dogs came from the direction he had taken.

As the long night softened into day, the two men began to run. David ran for his life without looking back. He ran until the faint noises of the camp disappeared. He ran until he was aware only of the sound of his own feet pounding the dirt, crunching sticks and leaves. He ran until he could not run any further, and then he kept running still.

He was twenty-eight years old.

He had one mission from then on. He would alert as many Jews as possible to what was happening. He imagined that they would listen to him in shock, and then gather their most essential belongings and flee. He could save men, women, children. Grandfathers, aunties, babies. Where would they go? That wasn't for him to work out. It was only for him to warn them.

Eventually, he would indeed travel to several towns telling his story. But hardly anyone heeded him, or the news he had to impart. When he said that many thousands of Jews were killed in the four days he had been at Treblinka, some thought he was crazy, a fantasist, touched. Others pretended to listen, but he could tell by the way they nodded their heads that they were hearing only his words and not the message. They would not do anything differently. They would not pack up their possessions. They would stay where they were. Their doubt was too great.

One man, however, sought David out. Dolfie Blumenstock had learned of this daring escape from his eldest son, but he wanted to hear the account firsthand. When Dolfie met David – travelling two hours by bus to do so – he knew that these were not made-up stories. David's descriptions were too detailed, his eyes too scared, his words too urgent. He recounted events that sounded unbelievable – could invalids really have been thrown onto fires? – but Dolfie believed every word. He raced home to his wife, who had never seen him so pale nor so worried. 'Genya,' he said to her, 'our prayers have not saved us. God cannot save us. It is time for us to save ourselves.'

Dolfie's encounter with David had forever altered him. What neither man could have known at the time was the extent to which this brief meeting would impact them both, bonding the two in a way that would change not just their lives but the course of both their personal histories.

One

Melbourne, Australia, 2017

Later, it would be hard to erase the memory of how my mother looked in her last weeks. Appearance had always mattered to her, not so much for vanity's sake but because the effort was important. For as long as I could remember, Mira performed the same ritual before she went out. Standing in front of the mirror, there would be a final application of coral-red lipstick, a patting-down of her outfit, one last spritz of hairspray over her hair, already teased into a stiff bouffant. The scent of that spray – Schwarzkopf's Taft – always transported me back to the days when I would tug on her jacket as a five-year-old and command: 'Hair.' With that, my mother would bend down and let me sniff her head. I'd inhale giddily, the sharp strands tickling my nose, then exhale with satisfaction. 'Ahhh.' My mother, who had worked as a fit model in Paris when she lived there in the 1950s, was always beautiful, almost until the end. But not at the end.

In those final weeks, I could hardly recognise Mira as she sat in her sunken, worn recliner. Her blonde coiffure, modelled on an icy Hitchcockian heroine, had turned to grey, and had become so sparse and patchy that she now wore a turban to cover it. Her headwear was bright and colourful, but she was not. Her skin had also turned greyish, and although she had once gone to the hairdresser and worn lipstick before appointments with her oncologist, she now no longer bothered to put her dentures in, so that her mouth fell slack, unsmiling. She nodded when her grandchildren walked into the room, but her gaiety had been packed away long before, like a suitcase of maternity clothes when you've finished having babies.

A few months earlier, the illness held her in a looser grip. She had lost some hair, she was slower to move, but at least her voice was recognisably hers. It might not have been as singsongy as it once was, but it wasn't yet a flat drawl. It was more like a discordant piano key pressed occasionally. And if her smile was no longer a constant, it was still there to be prompted.

But each day a little more of her Mira-ness became covered up. Fewer things gave her pleasure. Not television, which gave her a headache, although she kept the sound on as a kind of white noise. Not music, even though she was the sort of person who'd always woken up singing invented songs. '*Birdelah, tzipitzah*,' her father used to call out to her when day broke in her childhood home in Czechoslovakia. She had told me that his nicknames translated to 'little bird'. He was known for his singing, too.

During that period, I would turn up at her house with artificial cheer, bringing whatever I could to make her day easier. Sometimes, this was vegetable soup that I had cooked, although her appetite had waned. Occasionally, I came with home aids, handing her a non-slip bath mat or a therapeutic pillow with a flourish, as if proffering a bunch of flowers. Or I summoned the odd expert: a meditation teacher who gave her a mantra; a chiropractor who used a little spring-loaded instrument on her back, each pump making a noise like a toy gun. She allowed these people to offer their services, nodding politely when they arrived. But once they left, she would breathe out in relief.

Often, I would find someone already there with her – my brother, Fred, who took care of the administrative details and paperwork that kept multiplying, or my eldest sister, Jeannette, who had to drive for nearly an hour to see our mother. Jeannette lived in Woop Woop, according to Mira, since her suburban property masqueraded as a rural one, with kangaroos bounding across the grass and from time to time a snake slithering by.

Ordinarily my sister was the late one, arriving breathless at our Friday night Shabbat dinners as the wine was being poured, a half-hour after everyone else. But once the three of us decided on attending each of Mira's medical appointments, Jeannette was never late to anything.

In the bland offices of oncologists and physicians and surgeons, she would ask the medical questions, tossing around scientific jargon with ease. I was the note keeper, recording whatever the doctor said with two quick thumbs on my phone, a jumble of words I transcribed without listening to, ensuring I had enough information to later relay to Lilianne, our sister in the US. Fred was the one who sat there with quiet authority, making my mother smile with a joke in the waiting room, calming her with his dependability.

When Mira's condition deteriorated, we made a roster to ensure that one of us was always with her around the clock, even when nursing staff were present as well. My mother insisted on dying in her home, and so it was there she declined, largely in the lounge room so filled with her touches. Not much had been changed since a 1970s interior freshen-up, and I knew the position and provenance of each little tchotchke. The Lalique crystal flower sat on the coffee table, a present from my mother's friend Lily. On the TV cabinet, a tiny silver ice-cream cart, its lids connected by delicate chains, bought by my late father in Rome when I was thirteen – my first overseas holiday.

My mother's imprint was everywhere: in the damask-flocked wallpaper that I would run my fingers over as a child, feeling the velvety bumps beneath my fingertips, and in the faded embroidery of her foot stool, with its brass claw legs. She was prone to decorating with vivid colours, and I was with her when she purchased a chaise longue at an auction and promptly had it reupholstered in deep purple velvet. Not one to waste anything, she turned the extra scraps of fabric into a rectangular pillow and fashioned it as a bear, using even smaller fabric pieces for its eyes and ears.

Her rumpus room boasted two separate wallpaper patterns in matching colours, a kaleidoscopic rainbow in electric hues of blue, green and yellow. On one wall, the colours formed huge ovals; opposite it, the same shades in vertical lines. To walk into that part of the house was to enter a psychedelic vortex, and although I thought it something of an eyesore when I was a teenager, by the time I was grown, visitors with a design bent would be impressed. A friend of mine joked that I shouldn't invite the owner of a mid-century modern furniture store inside: 'He would have a field day. He'd strip all of this from top to bottom.' If my mother had overheard that remark, she would have nodded in agreement. She had confidence in her taste.

Now all of my childhood memories had got mixed up with the present day, which carried the smell of antiseptic and medicine and illness. I could no longer enter Mira's kitchen and conjure up her almond horseshoe biscuits, which she sometimes shaped into the first letters of my children's names when they baked with her. Instead, I'd see the line-up of drugs: vials of ugly tablets in various sizes, sitting alongside copious instructions handwritten by Jeannette. You couldn't forget to administer any of them because the consequences were dire; instead of just worrying about her ovarian cancer, we had to hope that we could keep Mira's tumour from growing lest she die of a bowel obstruction instead. My mother, who had once treated herself to daily pastries when she lived in Paris and could never resist the lure of a boiled lolly, no longer wanted to eat a thing. The clothes she wore became looser, gathering in folds around her as her body shrank.

But there was an element of her illness that wasn't so terrible, as I got to feed her soup by the spoonful, and dab her face with a warm cloth. The sicker she grew, the more she hated to depend on others to do these things. Yet the more childlike she became in her dependency, losing the ability to control her body and its functions, the more tenderly I felt towards her. When she slept, I'd stroke her hand gently, her nails always beautifully polished, her silver wedding ring still on – she was allergic to gold – and I'd remember that she had done the same for me when I was a small child. My real appreciation for her mothering had come to me late, after I had children of my own. Recently, I found a letter I wrote to her in her last year:

> I truly believe that as children, we pick our parents. That somewhere, our souls are up in the sky, choosing the very best parents for us: ones who will teach us what we need to be taught, and who are the exact right fit for the exact path we are meant to follow. There's no other explanation, anyway – how did I get so lucky to have you as a mother? I must have pushed everyone else out of the line to get to you first.

* * *

Mira had always seen herself as a lucky person too, which was unfathomable given all that she'd been through. She spoke of her luck as a constant, even an attribute – like having a good memory. She would go to the Crown Casino's Mahogany Room and plan to spend a hundred dollars on roulette until she lost. She never lost. 'I'm a lucky player,' she said, and it's what my father said about her too, every time she beat him at a hand of Red Aces, the card game they played nightly, endlessly.

So when cancer struck, she couldn't believe it. She actually couldn't think of a plausible reason as to why she, of all her family members, should get cancer, and she would rack her brains for a precedent. 'No one in my family ever had cancer,' she would say, forgetting that hardly anyone in her family had lived long enough to get it.

* * *

When she fell ill, it was a surprise to us all, given how stoic and energetic she was. I don't remember her ever taking to bed with a cold, but when she started going for regular afternoon *shlufs*, or sleeps, we figured that's what women in their late eighties did. But then she complained of pain when she walked, and she so rarely had pain, and then she went to the doctor, when she almost never went to the doctor.

After the first visit, Jeannette was hopeful. 'It looks like it could be diverticulosis,' she pronounced, 'which is treatable. That's good.' She didn't say what it might be if it was bad. We all waited and hoped.

The night before Mira received her definitive test results, I took her to the opening night party of a costume exhibit at Rippon Lea Estate, a heritage homestead set on fourteen acres of land, lush with foliage and, that night, awash with people. It was her eighty-eighth birthday, and I had packed a folding wheelchair in my car in case she needed it. She didn't look sick. She remained seated for most of the night, but she nodded at strangers and smiled in her regal way as if she were the hostess who had graciously allowed people into her domain. They smiled back. Strangers were always taken with her. She stopped a well-known fashion editor who brushed past her, and admired her checked navy-and-white trench coat, feeling the fabric between two fingers. I could see that this editor was impressed with my mother's eye, and flattered by her attention. On this evening, with the mother I had always known, I tried to absorb all the details: the crisp night air, the 1920s beaded costumes, the tinkling laughter around us. I knew that everything might change the next day, that there was a chance this evening would act as a delineation between Before and After. If there was to be an After, I wanted to always remember the Before.

And when the next day came and the oncologist said solemnly that, yes, Mira had ovarian cancer, stage 3B, we all sat there dully, as stunned as she was. There weren't any tears or upset voices. As usual, my mother was matter-of-fact. 'You tell us what we have to do, doctor,' she said formally, in a way that belied her inherent stubbornness and resistance to doing what she was told, especially by doctors.

Months later, when she underwent round after round of chemotherapy, she would be decisive about the protocol. She refused the recommended amount of carboplatin, and so we asked the doctors to halve the dose, which proved the correct choice when the cancer's growth was halted for a time, while still leaving her well enough to go about her daily tasks. Even in the hospital ward, where she had monthly appointments, she insisted on hand-picking the nurse who would insert the port into her arm then drip-feed the chemo down a thin tube. 'I don't want *that* nurse,' she would whisper, pointing with her chin. 'They butchered me last time.' And she would show her bruises as proof.

She managed to say what she wanted directly but inoffensively; if that nurse had overheard her, they might have laughed, because there was something about Mira's delivery that presumed good humour even when the message was sharp. Months later, we found a top surgeon who agreed to operate on her tumour, believing he might be able to remove or reduce it. He was clear that it would not save her life, only prolong it. 'Listen, doctor,' she said, 'I do not want to die on the operating table. I don't want it.' He agreed. She tempered her words with a smile. People admired her forthrightness. People did her bidding; it was a talent she possessed.

The four of us spent so much time at sessions like these that my siblings and I started to develop a fondness for them, as if they were family catch-ups, and we had chosen a hospital for our location. We would banter together, batting small asides back and forth until they became running jokes, like we were kids teasing each other in the back of my mother's white Valiant on a long drive. On these occasions, Mira never looked weary, like the other patients. Instead, she was propped up on pillows, keeping up a continuous commentary on everything that was happening around her. We always left those sessions feeling hopeful, convinced that the medicine was working. And for a considerable period, when her tumour shrunk to less than half its size, it was.

* * *

Every few months came small changes, so imperceptible in the landscape that you didn't see them accumulating. The bathroom was altered to include a handrail, because Mira was no longer so steady on her feet. She stopped driving. An electric chair was put over the staircase, because the five stairs had become hazardous. She stopped cooking. Jeannette searched online for an apparatus that might lower my mother into her bathtub, because for forty years I'd never seen her take a shower; the sound of running faucets was a perennial in the mornings of my childhood. Appearances were kept up, and my children and I accompanied my mother to a wig store that largely catered to married Jewish women who needed to cover their hair. There she picked out a chestnut-coloured hairpiece, but the shade was too dark for her and it sat too stiffly on her head. Eventually it would be discarded with all the other rituals of daily life we'd always thought were permanent.

She was in the last six months of her life when Fred suggested I interview her. As a journalist, asking questions was what I did. It wasn't to learn her life story; I thought I already knew that, although I would be proved wrong. I wanted to distract her from the aches, the nausea, the tiredness. I wanted to distract myself from it too.

And there was this other thing: I wanted to be reminded of the mother I'd known all my life, who was cheery and vital and formidable. I wanted to have one of those moments again that happened so often in my past, when we both found something so funny that we'd actually double over laughing, bending at the waist with our hands resting on our thighs, and the only noises that came out of our throats were wheezy, gaspy exhales, because that's how we each laughed hard. I wanted to hear my mother say something impossibly hilarious, the way she seemed to do all through my twenties. At the time, I'd write it down and use it as material. When I published my first article while still in university, she was worried that I'd give up studying law, and said to me: 'A bird in hand is worth more than a cow on the roof!' I wanted to be furious, but all I could do was giggle, and then repeat it to everyone umpteen times until it became part of my family's vernacular. I wanted to remind myself that this sick, tired, old lady was still my effervescent mother: good-humoured and intelligent and intrepid, the one who could speak seven languages fluently and had lived in several countries before making Australia home.

I had not ever interviewed a family member this way. When I conversed with subjects for magazines and newspapers, I held a list of questions in my head, hoping to squeeze them all in during my allotted time. The more famous the person I was interviewing, the less time I had; I was once given five minutes with a movie star for a cover story. With my mother, there was a time limit too: I didn't know how the days would progress or when her energy might flag. And I wasn't accustomed to interviewing my mother, especially not this version of her.

But after three decades of doing this job, I knew that asking questions wasn't the important part. Listening was. I had learned to hear the pauses taken between words, to notice where sentences cracked in the middle. I could pick up the excitement in someone's voice because I'd hit upon a topic they liked talking about, and I would note the faint sibilant sounds when childhood speech therapy hadn't entirely worked. I had learned to listen closely.

I started casually, perhaps lazily, stretching as far back as I could think of. 'What was it like, growing up in your home, before the war?' And so we began.

Two

A photograph of Mira's parents was on permanent display in my childhood home. Her mother – small-framed, buxom and straight-backed – gazing at the camera with seriousness and perhaps a touch of hidden defiance. Her look conjures up the image of a Gibson Girl portrait with her rounded face, pointed chin, poised expression and loosely piled-up hair. Mira's father, handsome and fairer, the tiniest trace of a smile at the edges of his mouth. He has the appearance of a moustachioed matinee idol, with perfectly even features and hair slicked to the side. They are each undeniably attractive.

Eugenia Sheindl Goldmann, known to everyone as Genya, was born in the mountainous village of Krościenko, now part of Poland, in 1892 while Abraham Yoel Blumenstock – 'Dolfie' – was born in 1885 in the picturesque former mining town of Banská Štiavnica, now in Slovakia. Genya's parents moved to the tiny, scenic village of Spišská Stará Ves, which looked out to the Pieniny mountain range and was close to the Dunajec River. It was so small that my mother would later joke that it wasn't included on maps of the area; it was as pint-sized as a postage stamp in a bag filled with letters. Its population numbered slightly over 1200 when Genya was coming of age, and it must have been idyllic for her family, with a quarter of its residents being Jewish. The town was primarily made up of one very long main street, but it was densely packed with buildings: stores in the front, and brick homes in the rear.

It was easy to picture the bustling *kehilla*, or congregation, that had begun forming there in the early eighteenth century. Spišská Stará Ves included many of the institutions considered vital for a Jewish community to flourish: a small synagogue, set a little back on the town's main road, that was simple but elegant. A Jewish cemetery, where the newer gravestones were very plain, with limited ornamentation and some Hebrew writing. There was also a *Chevra Kadisha*, or Jewish burial society, and a *mikvah*, the Jewish bathhouse which both men and women are required to attend separately for ritual cleansing on specified occasions.

The *mikvahs* of Eastern Europe were typically subterranean, stone-walled structures, with a bathing cavity at their centre. The one in my mother's town was adjacent to the synagogue, tucked away and out of sight in the building where the rabbi and other Jewish functionaries – the *chazzan*, or cantor, who led the prayers in song, and the *gabbai*, who assisted with services – all lived on separate floors. It would have seemed unchanged since medieval times: modest in appearance, and filled with water that at least partially came from a 'living' source, such as natural springs. Rivers that dried up in summer could not be used, because they might be filled with rainwater, which is considered stagnant, and are not inherently Divine for the ritual that takes place. The literal translation of the word '*mikvah*' is 'collection', because in the Old Testament, God collected all the waters of the earth together, parting them from land.

Mikvahs are holy places: it is impossible to step into one without feeling the pull of Judaism's ancient history and the reverence of what is involved. They were not traditionally places of luxury, but nevertheless a luxury of spirituality is invoked. Those who enter must be completely clean before immersing themselves in the warm waters, removing jewellery and, in the modern day, even nail polish, so that there's no barrier between the person and the living waters – because the purpose of the *mikvah* isn't to physically cleanse the body; it is to purify the soul.

Jewish law dictates that a *mikvah* is more important than even a synagogue, and if there is a choice, the hallowed Torah scrolls must be sold to raise funds for building one. It is the touchstone of married life: after a woman's menstrual period, she cannot touch her husband for seven days, nor he her. At the end of that week, after visiting the *mikvah*, they can resume marital relations. The *mikvah*'s very existence in Spišská Stará Ves said much about the *Yiddishkeit* among the Jewish population, the sense of Jewishness ingrained in their souls.

The town also had its own *shochet* – the kosher slaughterer prescribed by Jewish law, since meat can only be eaten when the animal has been killed in a swift, painless way – and two kosher butcheries. It was in one of these butcheries that Mira's parents first met; Genya's parents owned it, and she worked there. Dolfie was passing through the village one day – Spišská Stará Ves was a thoroughfare for people taking their wares to other towns to sell – and walked into the butchery. He was immediately struck by the young woman who served him, so shy that she couldn't look him in the eye when he gave her his order. He suspected she also felt the immediate thrum of connection between them, since she turned bright red on his approach.

This was unusual for the day. Young Jewish couples had no expectation of meeting this way, as nearly all of them were introduced through a *shadchan*, or professional matchmaker. Marriage had a transactional element to it: a dowry was settled upon, and families would agree to combine. But Genya's family already did things a little differently; her brother Samuel refused a dowry from his bride's family when they fell in love, even though his prospective in-laws had a lucrative jewellery business and he himself was struggling. That's how they were in her family: when they fell in love, that was it.

It is easy to imagine Dolfie feeling emboldened by Genya's shyness, and returning soon afterwards in search of another interaction. Did he dare to brush his finger over her hand when she passed him his food packages, or hold her gaze for a moment too long, once she overcame her reserve? There would have been no illicit meetings for this pair: they were too well brought up, too respectful of their familial and religious constraints. But they were nevertheless independent thinkers, and neither of them felt bound so strongly by the rules that had been laid out for them. They agreed to go for a walk together, then another. At some point, an exchange took place between them, where Dolfie proposed, and Genya accepted.

A love match might have been frowned upon, but they were the appropriate age for marriage: she was twenty-one; he twenty-eight. Still, social norms needed to be followed, and so Dolfie's father ventured to Spišská Stará Ves to greet his future daughter-in-law. The meeting got off to a bad start: Dolfie's father was a man of rigorous faith, and didn't believe his future *mechutanim*, the parents of his potential daughter-in-law, to be quite as *frum*, or observant, as he. But he was a practical man, too, so just in case Genya's parents didn't observe the laws of *kashrut* – kosher – strictly enough, he brought with him all of his own ceramic plates, as well as several pots and pans, ensuring that none of his food would be touched by the potentially non-kosher dishes in their house.

When he met Genya, he instantly approved of her, although he did have one condition that needed to be met. 'She has to wear a *sheitel*!' the old man decreed, meaning that she must cover her hair under the marriage wig that observant women wore, since her own hair was considered akin to nakedness and for a husband's viewing alone. Genya wasn't thrilled with the idea – not many women in her town subscribed to this law – but she was in love with Dolfie, so she could make this compromise.

She would not wear a *sheitel* for long. World War I broke out after they married, and Dolfie was enlisted in the Austro-Hungarian army. He was given work as a translator, but made a good impression on the major in charge when it was discovered that he was skilled at a popular yet complicated card game called Mariáš. Soon, Dolfie was awarded extra privileges, and his young wife was allowed to visit. Genya duly arrived at the army barracks one day. She wore a new dress for the occasion and – because she was so pale-skinned yet eschewed make-up – pinched her cheeks until her eyes smarted, so that the twin dots of blush brought her youth to the fore. Not knowing where to go, she asked a soldier, 'Can you tell me where I can find Mr Blumenstock?' The man gave a shout in Dolfie's direction. 'Hey, Blumenstock! Your mother is here!' The hairpiece that Genya wore wasn't natural-looking like the wigs of today; it had aged her by at least two decades. Embarrassed, she pulled it off there and then. 'Promise or no promise, I'll never wear this again,' she declared.

The pair struggled financially in their early years of married life in Spišská Stará Ves. At first, Dolfie made his trade buying trees from people who owned large swathes of forest, arranging for them to be cut down and the wood sold to furniture manufacturers. The logs were shipped on a barge that floated along the Dunajec River to Danzig, before being transported into Poland, and it was a prosperous enterprise until one day there was a great storm, and the enormous heft of wood was almost completely washed away. Dolfie, who still had money owing to the woodcutters, the delivery men and so forth, was left out of pocket. Poland's steep inflation also served to undermine Dolfie's forestry business, so he supplemented his income by buying shoes from a factory and reselling them at fairs. With his profits, he bought a shop which sold fabric and haberdashery and had a residence at its rear. Genya sewed clothes to sell in the store and Dolfie kept working in the tree business, juggling two jobs to support his growing family.

The couple eventually had five children: Armin (nicknamed Heshek) born in 1914, Olga in 1916, Alexander (known as Shani) in 1921, Simon (called Yanchi by the family) in 1924, and Miriam, forever dubbed 'Mira', the youngest, born in 1927. The two girls favoured their mother in looks, sporting Genya's deep dimples. The boys all had light-coloured eyes – Shani's were bright blue – and might have been mistaken as German by a foreigner, since that was the primary language they spoke at home. Slovak was only spoken by the children at school.

Although Mira remembered the family's occasional financial difficulties – when Dolfie was unable to pay some suppliers, he handed out tickets to be used in the haberdashery store, and in a bad week only those redeemed IOU papers sat in the cash register – their fortunes steadily improved. They were neither wealthy nor poor, but managed well with what they had, even employing a maid who helped Genya with the cleaning and occasional child-minding.

For the five Blumenstock children, life was filled with sweet pleasures. Their grandmother Chava, Genya's mother, resided close by in town. Her husband had died of a sudden tetanus infection in 1928, a year after Mira was born, and so her eldest son, Samuel, and daughter-in-law Klara lived with her. When her grandchildren let themselves into her house, they would immediately be hit by the waft of sugary baked goods, since Chava kept a cupboard near her front door stocked with biscuits and cakes. They had only to turn the knob to find within a babka pastry, heaving with chocolate and dusted with the faintest layer of sugar, or a plaited yeast cake stuffed with crushed almonds. They indulged whenever they visited, and were often slipped the occasional gift as well.

Mira was a curious and independent child, and after her father visited synagogue on Shabbat, she would ask him to share whatever *parsha*, or passage in Jewish scripture, the rabbi had read that week. Dolfie would bring down from his shelves a thick book containing the *Chumash*, the bound form of the Pentateuch, the Hebrew Bible. The Hebrew was supplemented with Yiddish translations, and Mira pored over it until she understood the words for herself. A few years later, she would become an enthusiastic member of Bnei Akiva, the Zionistic youth group.

Genya, a loving mother, ruled with a quiet authority rather than a firm hand. The only time the children remembered her getting upset was when the two youngest boys – eight and eleven at the time – were playing a game of cops and robbers, with their five-year-old baby sister as the bad guy. Their game took place in one of the house's rooms with the door closed. The boys got angry at each other, and their playful roughhousing turned into a more heated fight. Suddenly, Genya appeared in the doorway. 'My children are hurting each other?' she asked, shocked. 'How can my children do that?' Her eyes glistened, watery with tears. Mira later said she had never heard so much sorrow in her mother's voice. All three children burst out crying themselves at the sight and ran to her. 'Mama, we're sorry! We will never do it again.' They all knew how sensitive their mother was.

And still so very shy, even with her family. Sometimes Dolfie would fail to recall the words of a song, and he would turn to his wife for help. 'Genya, I'm sure you remember it. Sing that song for me.' Instantly, Genya's face would become red – 'like paprika', Mira said – but she would want to please her husband too. And so she would sing, in her melodious voice.

The townspeople who patronised their store respected her, responding to her kindness, her gentle manner. She listened and nodded as they gossiped or confided in her. And she always kept busy, her hands never still, using the scraps of leftover fabric to make other, smaller items, such as an apron or a shirt. She did not begrudge the amount of work to be done, even when her husband occasionally gambled – and lost – at cards in the neighbourhood coffee house. It wasn't a large amount since he played only for his own amusement. If he returned home with his pockets slightly emptier, his wife didn't make a fuss, but was resourceful instead. 'Don't worry – I'll make an extra shirt to cover your losses,' she would say. She was never resentful, and the two never argued.

Genya liked her children to be well presented, and dressed them accordingly, often sewing exquisite garments herself. For the store, she used her children in place of a tailor's dummy, and one day asked eight-year-old Mira to try on an elaborate dress which she said she was custom-making for a girl who was a similar size. Mira fingered the delicate gossamer between her fingers, both admiring and coveting the polka-dotted fabric and its puff sleeves, the stiff pouf skirt. It was too much for her to bear. 'Why do you make such beautiful clothes for the shop and for customers, and not for me?' she asked petulantly. A few months later, when it was Mira's birthday, she unwrapped the present from her parents, packaged in layers of soft tissue. The dress lay there, as charming as ever, 'and I nearly fainted', remembered Mira many years later. 'It was something incredible.' She loved that dress, white with a rainbow of coloured spots, knowing that its gathers were sewn so carefully by her diligent mother, who had intended it for her daughter all along.

Three

When I interviewed Mira, I did so in brief sittings, making sure I did not tire her out or overwhelm her. She was already too weary to stay seated at the dinner table for the duration of our Friday night Sabbath meal, so once she retired to the adjoining lounge room, I began with my questions.

During one of our first sessions, she related an anecdote I had never heard before. I had always presumed that my mother's childhood was bleak and austere, since she grew up in Eastern Europe at the time of World War II. But then it emerged that her parents were avid theatre-goers, and would see a musical performance whenever one was in town, their two daughters and three sons in tow. After each show, the family would come home and retire to their bedrooms, which were situated around a communal kitchen area — the parents in theirs, the brothers in one, the sisters in another. From their darkened rooms, someone would start singing a tune they recalled from that day's performance. Of course, their memories weren't perfect, so soon another family member would chime in, and then another, all trying to fill in the gaps. They would do this with every song they could remember, until a chorus of voices and laughter and harmonies filled the space, overlapping each other, words remembered and misremembered, the reprise becoming almost as sweet and memorable as the show itself.

This story brought me to tears, as it explained so much. When I was a teenager, my friends often commented on my mother's sunny demeanour, her ready smile. I noticed it years later, too, when I was a twenty-something living in Manhattan, and she came to visit. I marvelled at how she was able to coax even the gruffest New Yorker into their best behaviour. How did she manage all this, when she had been exposed to the horrors of war? When I realised she had been brought up in a house of song and joy, it made more sense to me; it was like finding the missing piece of a jigsaw puzzle that finally fit.

* * *

As her days became punctuated by the hallmarks of illness and its associated pains, our goal became to make our mother comfortable, although she often was not. Mira had never been a good sleeper, subsisting on five or so hours a night, but once cancer took hold, even that sleep became broken and restless. If I was close by when she woke, I would ask her hopefully, 'Did you dream about anything special?' I knew that she sometimes dreamed of her late mother, which would bring her much comfort whenever it occurred. It was more than a reminder of the way Genya looked or how she spoke: Mira had always believed that the dead could communicate with the living, and even at the age of eighty-nine she would try to summon some maternal solace on the nights she felt troubled. She would go to bed and close her eyes tightly, trying to free her mind from whirring thoughts. I guess it was a prayer of sorts, but she would often tell me that she would lie there until a feeling of wellbeing swept over her, and she was certain that her mother's spirit was nearby, whispering in her ear, '*Ich bin mit dir.*' I am with you.

I readily understood the devotion of a mother's love. Holidaying in Bangkok in 1992, having just turned twenty-six, I was a passenger in a motorised tuk-tuk that collided with a car. It was Saturday in Melbourne, and Mira was observing the Sabbath, exchanging her usual bustle for a day of rest. When she received the phone call from the Thai hospital I was taken to, she put aside the religious laws of Shabbat, frantically catching both taxi and then plane to be by my side the next morning. There, she took one look at me – my face knotted in pain – and gave the nurses brisk instructions. Soon I was moved to a room with an air conditioner, and the doctor who would later perform a dozen surgeries on me back in Australia said that without the room switch, the infection in my leg would have become life-threatening.

Still, in those early hours after my accident, it wasn't gratitude that I was feeling. 'Why me?' I asked my mother, a woman who had experienced so much hardship in her own life that the thoughtlessness of my question would later shame me. But Mira was always sympathetic, always considering the other person's point of view, even when I dared to continue: 'Why me, when you always tell me that your parents are looking out for me?' It was a rebuke, I knew, and she would have been right to answer sharply. Instead, her response was simple. 'I don't know where they were,' she said. She too was puzzled.

Until, that is, she had a dream. It took place in the afternoon, several hours after she arrived, while she was sleeping by my side in a fold-out bed, exhausted by her panicked journey. When she woke, it was clear that this dream was memorable for its realistic detail. Walking to the window of the small room, she peered out. 'Did your accident happen here, right outside?' she asked. It had, strangely enough: the tuk-tuk came to a stop – with me pinned underneath it – at the threshold of the local hospital. I was not sure how she could have known that, and it was such an unlikely location: already within footsteps of medical care. 'In my dream, I watched it happen,' she said. I wondered what that meant. Had she seen the way the tuk-tuk's metal bar twisted like it was rubber? Or the skin of my leg slowly rip open, like a banana peel revealing the soft fruit within? 'I saw that my parents were there with you, and they intervened to save your life,' she added.

It was impossible to believe, but still: doctors were always astounded that the accident hadn't resulted in my paralysis or death. My mother fervently believed that the spirits of my grandparents had been there that day. I wanted to think so too. But at that age, I had not yet learned to be grateful for what I had. I was too busy focusing on all that had gone wrong.

Four

Mira's father had been given the Hebrew name of Abraham, but the Germanic version of his name was Adolf, so his family called him Dolfie. If Genya brought calm into the house, he brought music. As soon as he woke up in the morning, there was a melody on his tongue, and he would sing throughout the day, his temperament set to permanent optimism. There was no doubt he had been born with a musical gift, and he played the violin proficiently. All his children had wonderful voices, but it was little Mira who expressed this talent with abandon; in the evenings they would sing, link arms and dance in circles around the kitchen together, both of them caught up in joy.

Dolfie delighted in teaching his youngest Yiddish songs, trotting Mira out to perform for guests, or sometimes taking her to sing at other people's *simchas*: a wedding, a bar mitzvah. She would stand on a table, this little twig of a girl, not a speck of her mother's shyness in her, and her voice would fill the room. She became known for it in her small town, so that whenever she passed the local inn, its owner Mrs Mangel would offer her a trade. 'Mira, would you like to have a biscuit? If you sing, I will give you one.' And she would do so, enjoying the spotlight as much as the treat she'd earned.

But it was Dolfie she most wanted to please, and it was clear that he was very proud of her: of her confidence, her intelligence, her independence. When they walked together, she would try to keep in step with him, taking as big a stride as he did, and he would laugh merrily at her game. He was not someone who craved solitude, and so when he went for his evening walks, and the other members of his family said it was too snowy or rainy to accompany him, he was grateful to have Mira by his side. She secretly suspected she was his favourite, and maybe she did occupy that special place the youngest in families often fill.

There was one regular walk that Mira did not join him on. Every Saturday, when Dolfie came home from synagogue after reciting the morning service, he would return home for lunch and a one-hour rest. Then, in the afternoon, he and Genya would go for a secluded walk – not into the town's centre, but rather behind it, where the streets gave way to verdant gardens and the mountains rose in the distance. It was normal to see a couple walking side by side, but Genya and Dolfie would hold hands, with Dolfie occasionally stopping to caress Genya's cheek. 'They were very, very happy,' said Mira. 'People in the town said, "They're already very old! How can they still be in love?" But they were. They were very much in love their whole lives.'

And Dolfie's wife understood him, catering to his idiosyncratic whims. For example: in their yard they kept one cow, specifically to provide the family with their own source of milk and butter. They could have bought those items in town, but Dolfie didn't trust the hygiene standards of anyone else; to that end, he would also make his children wash their cow's udders in warm water before milking her. During the war, he had been shot in the stomach, and it was hard for him to digest food properly thereafter. So while the rest of the family dined on rye bread, his portion alone was made from white dough.

Their large kitchen had two tables, allowing them to adhere strictly to the laws of kosher: one table was only for *milchig* (made with milk) food, the other for *fleishig* (meat), with the two never allowed together in the same meal. When they ate, Genya insisted on setting her table formally, using a white tablecloth even at midday. Lunch was, in fact, the main meal; the family's shop would close in the early afternoon for a break, opening again later. But the formalities ended with the tablecloth, as mealtimes were somewhat boisterous, with conversation and merriment whipping around the kitchen.

If Dolfie had any kind of reputation in town, it was for being a clever and foresighted man. Frequently, people would knock on the front door and ask him to step outside so they could seek his advice privately. 'When people had problems, they asked my father what he thought they should do, whether it was a personal or business decision,' said Mira. 'And people came very, very often.' He was also kind: if a neighbour could not pay for his goods, Dolfie covered the cost without question, handing him something extra from his larder: some homemade butter, some bottled preserves.

* * *

Theirs was a fairly simple life, characterised by a resolute practicality. A popular Yiddish proverb of the time – *Az me muz, ken men* – summed up the family's world view. *When one must, one can.* They did.

There was no electricity in their village until Mira turned nine, nor did they have running water in their home. Proper baths happened only once a month or so, requiring either the maid or the children to take one bucket after another from a distant outside pump and fill up their indoor tub, situated in a dark alcove in a corner of the house. Three of the family members would use the water consecutively before it was thrown out, and afterwards the tub needed to be drained. On the other days, the children each fetched a single bucket's worth of water from the stove, where some hot water was always kept for cooking. They would use that to scrub themselves with a washcloth: their feet, neck, ears, body. Only on rare occasions would the family splurge on rented baths, near the *mikvah*.

Many tasks were laborious. A washerwoman came to town once a month to do the family's washing; between times, a massive pile of dirty clothes would accumulate. The woman's job was to fetch the clothes, boil them in water and rinse them in the river. Afterwards, she would hang them on a line in their attic, but if conditions were icy, the clothes would stiffen in the air, sometimes taking weeks to dry completely.

When they were younger, the children's days were often spent helping out in the store. Mira had known how to cut and measure ribbon from the age of five, and Dolfie invented an ingenious system for marking the fabrics with prices. The first ten letters of their surname – B - L - U - M - E - N - S T - O - C – each represented a digit from one to ten, with B standing for one, and so on. Dolfie would write a coded 'price' on a roll of fabric; if it was marked 'UE', the children would know that the lowest price they could accept, after bargaining with the customer, was 35 Czechoslovak koruna. It was an effective method, devised so that the younger ones knew how much they could allow customers to haggle. But more than that, it made them feel like they were part of a secret club, in which they were smart and quick and inventive.

* * *

Reading was not a luxury in Mira's house but a given, with books frequently borrowed from the library. Dolfie would read the newspaper, sharing the news of the day with his family over dinner. Genya was an avid consumer of romance fiction, her eyes widening when she found something riveting. Curiosity got the better of Mira, who snuck one of her novels away, reading it surreptitiously under her bedcover. When Genya caught her, she said, 'That's not a book for you!' But Mira found nothing wrong with the sordid tale of a working-class woman, her drunkard husband and their daughter who was forced to turn to prostitution. All the children read voraciously, although Yanchi loved comic books the best, waiting impatiently for the next instalment to arrive.

Mira had another source for books: one of the town's Jewish lawyers was also her *madrich*, or leader, at Bnei Akiva, and he famously spent most of his income expanding his home library. The bookshelves stretched from floor to ceiling, with the books arranged in alphabetical order. To Mira this represented unimaginable riches. The *madrich* allowed her to borrow whatever book she wanted on one condition: when she finished it, he would quiz her on its contents and ask her to critique it. It thrilled Mira to be pushed intellectually this way; she would always remember this man as a great educator.

Education was considered a necessity, but despite being at the top of her class, Mira already knew that she should keep her aspirations modest. Everyone told her she would make a good teacher, and that seemed ambitious enough. Her routine was to go to the public school in the morning – starting at 8 a.m. and finishing by 1 p.m. – and attend *cheder*, which taught Jewish history and learning, two afternoons a week.

Shani was especially academically gifted, and in later years his teachers urged the family to send him to a gymnasium – or secondary school – in the nearby city of Kežmarok, since there was no local high school that could prepare him for university. Shani moved accordingly and stayed at the home of his aunt and uncle, Roza and Gerson Storch. Roza was Genya's sister, and Shani was friendly with his three male cousins, the youngest of whom – Kurt – was three years younger than Mira. But it was an experiment that ended badly. Shani found the city's attractions more alluring than study, and he would routinely sell his schoolbooks in order to take out pretty girls. At the end of the year, he failed his subjects and had to return home.

Outside of school and work, the Blumenstock children had plenty of time to play games such as marbles and draughts. One could often find a chalked hopscotch-type outline on the street, and team sports were popular: volleyball for Mira, soccer for her brothers. In summer, they went boating or played tennis on a stretch of lawn in front of the school. In winter, water was placed on the lawn's surface to convert it to a small ice-skating rink with lights strung up all around, making it a festive gathering spot. There was also skiing and tobogganing, the latter usually done on old bits of wood fashioned to hold a child or two.

One day, Heshek – who was by then working full-time with his father – came home with a present for his little sister: a shop-bought toboggan, shiny and incredibly beautiful, complete with an actual seat and carved handles at the top. Everybody admired it. Later that winter, when Shani asked to borrow it, Mira unhesitatingly agreed. She was philosophical about the outcome when Shani promptly had an accident and the toboggan ended up in small pieces. 'No more toboggan!' she said with a laugh when recounting that incident. If she regretted its loss – if she ever imagined what it would have been like to experience hours of merriment on the snowy hills riding that well-crafted carriage while all her friends rode their plain, makeshift ones – she never said so.

* * *

The Blumenstocks were happy with their lives. They lived comfortably and socialised easily; they loved each other and the parents were inordinately proud of their offspring. Often, Genya would turn to her husband and exclaim: 'Have a look, Dolfie! Have a look at our children! One more beautiful than the other! One more clever than the other! We are so lucky to have children like that.' Dolfie would turn that into a joke: 'Yes,' he'd say. 'We should start a circus. One of them sings. One of them plays an instrument. The third one is an acrobat. With our children, we would make a lot of money with a circus.' It seemed there was no end to the things that amused them, no limit to the good fortune they enjoyed.

* * *

As Mira's daughter, I could recognise the aspects of her childhood that she retained in adulthood. She taught my son a complicated way of learning his times tables – it involved counting his knuckles and using other fingers as a bridge – which was so convoluted that he was the only one in the family who ever managed to learn it. She always appreciated the luxury of soaking in a bathtub. She was never without a book by the side of her bed. And she could often be heard singing snippets of long-ago Yiddish songs. Occasionally she would switch to old-fashioned tunes that had been popular before I was born, such as the vaudeville 'Ta-ra-ra Boom-de-ay', or Doris Day's 'Que Sera, Sera'.

She used ordinary skills in extraordinary ways. Having learned how to sew, she not only repaired clothes but created new garments without a pattern: a patchwork jumpsuit for me, a summer kaftan for herself. The jumpsuit was so soft and cosy that I wore it until holes began to appear on the knees, forcing her to cover them with patches, so reluctant was I to part with it. When I was in primary school, she made all of my fancy-dress costumes for the Jewish festival of Purim, leaning over her Singer machine for hours to produce something lively and creative. She gave me free rein to choose the designs and complied with my wishes: a pink satin top and matching balloon pants trimmed in purple braid à la *I Dream of Jeannie*, or a regal confection of periwinkle gauze and silver stars for Queen Esther, the festival's heroine. At the age of seven, I announced that I'd like to dress up as a bunny waitress, something I'd learned about from a news report on TV when Hugh Hefner opened his Playboy Club. She helped me fashion a drinks tray out of a piece of wood and plastic wine goblets, adding a pompom bunny tail to complete the look.

Her cheerful approach to the mundane made light of many disappointing events. If a stream washed an inflatable ball away on a summer holiday, she would laugh and say: 'Goodbye, Charlie!' If, as a recalcitrant child, I demanded another dessert after Mira had declared there to be no more, she would clap her hands together and declare: 'Finito, Mosquito!'

Sometimes I liked to imagine that not all of her childhood was lost. She found pieces of it through her own children, and perhaps those little stolen bits from the future managed to knit together the holes of the past.

Five

The eleven-year age difference between Mira and her sister Olga felt substantial to both of them. Within the family, Olga's best friend and co-conspirator was her brother Heshek, two years her senior, and the pair often seemed to exist in an exclusive bubble. When Mira was born, Olga was immediately jealous of her, and complained of feeling pushed aside when all the attention went to the newborn. Around the Passover Seder table that year, when she had drunk the requisite four tiny cups of wine, Olga grew tired and even a little tipsy. She suddenly announced, 'I am going to kill her! I don't want a sister!'

Like many older siblings, she was often required to take Mira along on her own outings, wheeling her in the family's much-used pram. By the time Mira's turn came, the pram was old and rickety, with a hole at its base. One warm afternoon, Olga met her friends at the creek, where they slipped off their shoes and paddled around. They left the pram at the water's edge, until one friend cried out, 'Olga! Mira is in the water!' The pram's hole had finally given way.

Through her siblings, Mira was able to see the courting rituals of the town's Jewish teenagers up close. Girls and boys flocked together in large groups, walking to the next town an hour away, where they knew the owners of a cafe and grocery store, and where biscuits would be laid out. Heshek and Shani flouted the rules of Sabbath by playing pool there on a Saturday.

Walking itself was often a social event, particularly on the weekend, when going on a 'corso' – known as 'promenading' in earlier eras – was a cause for great anticipation. Participants dressed up in their good clothes: the young men in dapper suits and ties, the women in loose, pleated dresses and, if they were feeling a little risqué, a skirt that revealed a hint of knee. The townspeople would meander along a stretch of footpath dotted with benches, nodding at each other as they passed. It was an opportunity for boys and girls to catch each other's eye and subtly flirt, but this wasn't an outing reserved merely for the young. The older people equally enjoyed the pastime, admiring the latest fashions, or noticing who among the youth had suddenly become head-turningly attractive.

If a Jewish boy and girl liked each other, they habitually went for walks with smaller groups of four or six, but never just alone with one another. The location was ideal for these strolls; Spišská Stará Ves had many picturesque spots along the river. Mushrooms could be foraged in the forest, and strawberries grew alongside hedgerows for the picking. Teenagers might hold hands when they were away from interfering adults, but if a young man wanted to court his intended, he visited her at home under her parents' supervision.

Heshek and Shani always had a different girl on their arms, but slender Olga, who looked so much like a grown version of Mira, did not have her sights set on anyone. In one photo of her, she wears a nurse's uniform, having learned first aid with her friends. They are all fetching and lithe, these women, but Olga's dimples gave her an extra appeal, making her appear both comely and good-humoured.

Perhaps it was due to the tight-knit nature of the Jewish community, or the strictness of their upbringing, but Mira could not remember a single Jewish girl who had become pregnant out of wedlock, although there were quite a few non-Jewish girls who had sudden weddings. If surface snapshots of village life created a picture of charming courtships, there was a shadowy side to being born into a small, insular town where codes of conduct were seldom broken, especially religious ones. Everyone remembered one dazzling couple who were palpably in love but, because one of them was divorced, the Catholic Church would not allow them to marry. They committed suicide side by side in the town's cemetery, deciding that if they could not live together, they would die together. It was one of the first real tragedies that Mira could recall, foreshadowing a time when the village would come to know a much greater collective darkness.

* * *

There were occasional childhood mishaps. When Mira was a baby, not yet able to roll over, the maid was asked to look after her for the day. But the maid had an errand to run, so she took Mira to the family store, leaving her underneath one of the large tables that were used for measuring giant pieces of material. Heshek, who at thirteen had recently been bar mitzvahed, was helping out, and he unknowingly knocked Mira with a bolt of fabric that was dragging on the ground. Suddenly a customer came running to Genya: 'Mrs Blumenstock, that baby is blue!' When Mira was picked up, she coughed and coughed and her colour returned. It became part of family lore, repeated over and over with amusement.

Another time, Mira recalled going to a Bnei Akiva camp with her brother Yanchi. The children played in a small body of water, catching little fish with the intention of eating them later. It didn't occur to the youngsters that fish needed to be refrigerated. The campers ate them, and were promptly felled with food poisoning; Yanchi could only lie down and groan. But Mira was spared: she hated that type of fish.

She would not be so lucky after she once went swimming in a lake, spending the entire day in freezing water. Feeling unwell when she finally emerged, her arms were stiff and achy by the time she got home. The doctor who was summoned put a fishy-smelling oil over her hands, wrapping them in a compress. The next day at school, all her classmates complained. 'Mira, that smells!' But it worked; the pain went away.

It was no wonder that she believed even the worst hurt would disappear, which is what happened one Friday night: it was still a short time away from dusk, when the Shabbat candles needed to be lit, and so the store was open, Genya tending to the last customer. Suddenly Genya remembered her chicken soup on the stove, bubbling away. 'Take it off the flame,' she instructed Mira, whose attempt to do so resulted in her dropping the boiling soup, spilling the hot liquid on her foot. Some of her skin peeled off, and this time the doctor was not so optimistic. 'Mira, you will have to wear special stockings, and I don't think the scar will ever go away.' But time passed, and the wound healed. You could never see the scar, even if you looked for it.

* * *

Two accidents stood out in my own childhood. I was nine years old, playing chasey at school, when I ran into another kid and crashed to the ground. Our family doctor sent me for an X-ray and said I had a torn ligament. Two weeks later, I still could not bear weight on it. 'You should make that child walk,' the doctor told my mother firmly. Mira's face flushed, her voice grew angry. 'There is something wrong with her!' she replied, and insisted on seeking a second opinion. Her instinct proved correct, as a small fracture eventually revealed itself. I was proud of my mother and the way she stood up for me against the doctor and all his medical knowledge.

And the previous year: I had needed thirteen stitches on the inside of my foot after pedalling on my sister Lilianne's brand-new exercise bicycle with no shoes on. Suddenly, my foot felt warm, and I saw blood everywhere. The sharp metal hinge covering the bike's chain had sliced my foot open with one of the revolutions. My mother took me to the emergency room at the Alfred Hospital, but was too shaky to give the formal consent that allowed the doctors to take me into surgery. 'I have to speak to her father first!' said Mira, even though she knew it would be hours before she could contact him.

Earlier that night, my father, Manny, had gone to a soccer match, a game he had anticipated for months. He was an avid soccer fan, watching Manchester United games on television, barracking loudly. But halfway through the match, a strange thing: he felt a sudden urge to leave. He wanted to resist it – surely he was being silly – but there was a sinking feeling he could not ignore, a sense of imminent danger. It had something to do with me, he felt strongly. 'I have to go,' he told his companion. 'There's something the matter with Rachi.' He sped home in his blue Holden, only to be greeted on the front steps by Lilianne, who directed him to the hospital. I often thought about that, too: the connection between parent and child being so fierce and immutable that it goes against everything else – logic, practicality, knowledge.

Six

Growing up, it was easy for Mira to tell when the Sabbath was approaching, even if she had lost track of time. Since it was a day when work was set aside – on that holy day, Jewish people did not cook, ride in carriages, write, conduct business transactions or kindle a fire, for example – the lead-up was marked by frenetic energy. To prepare, Genya and her mother, Chava, cooked together side by side, while Mira would peel the vegetables – always one of her daily chores – and help pat the dough for the chocolate rugelach pastries. She and her brothers would beg for a taste, standing by the kitchen bench until one of the women lost patience and popped a scrap of batter in their mouths.

From eighteen minutes before sundown on Friday until three stars appeared in the sky on Saturday evening, it was a day of rest. It was a time when the week's wrongs were righted and the family came together in prayer, song and food, their small house filled with odours of roasted meats and freshly baked cakes.

During the week, food would be simple: soup, perhaps, with a bit of homemade bread. But on Shabbat, meat was served, as well as other traditional Friday night dishes: rich, golden chicken soup, with small globules of fat swimming on the surface, together with handmade *lokshen*, or noodles. Beef brisket, cooked on top of onions which then became tender and caramelised, potatoes underneath seeping in the juices. A side of *farfel*, the small grain-like side dish made from egg noodles, cooked in oil until bits of it crisped up. Fruit compote for dessert. All of these would be served with the family's finest silverware in the large dining room – which, apart from having an expansive dining table, also housed a couch, fireplace and two beds, doubling as Dolfie and Genya's bedroom – rather than in the kitchen where they ate daily.

After dinner, no one left the table: Dolfie and his sons would sing *zemirot*, the Jewish hymns, in both Yiddish and Hebrew. Dolfie was a great fan of the Ukrainian cantor Josef 'Yossele' Rosenblatt, whom the *New York Times* called 'the Jewish Caruso', and preferred to sing the tunes of his arrangements. Mira thought that a seat at her Shabbat table was better than a ticket to the opera. The family's voices, coming together in harmony, were so uplifting and mellifluous that Mira would later say, 'The walls were trembling with the beauty of our songs.'

* * *

Even when she had a family of her own, Mira never really learned to enjoy cooking, despite easily filling a table with plates of heaving dishes. She preferred slow-cooked meals that she could place in the oven and forget about. Sometimes she would forget them completely: her palm would slap her forehead whenever she found a tray of roasted vegetables sitting atop the oven rack, long after dinner was finished and the plates had been washed and dried.

Regardless, her meals were famous among our family friends and relatives: they would remember her *cholent*, a stew of soft, smoked meat and bones so tender they melted into edible fragments, which must have reminded Mira of cooking with Genya each time she made it. Back then, the Blumenstocks would prepare this bean, pearl barley and meat casserole on Friday morning, taking it to the baker's brick oven to cook overnight, so that by the time it was Sabbath, the family could enjoy a hearty meal without having to light a fire themselves. My mother would also leave her oven on for twenty-four hours, keeping it on a very low temperature setting for the entire day. The *cholent* baked unattended until it was ready to eat, filling our house with a rich aroma that had our mouths watering from the moment we awoke.

When I was older, I noted Mira's cooking idiosyncrasies with amusement, as they often provided fodder for my writing. There was the way she cooked her vegetables, boiling them until they lost any shade of their bright colours. I marvelled at her ability to reach into frying pans of hot oil in order to fish something out with her fingers – she claimed her hands were so kitchen-inured that they didn't feel the heat – and wondered why she experimented with new recipes (hardly ever successfully) when her old ones were met with such enthusiasm. 'I get bored,' she would explain.

Some of these anecdotes would end up in print. When my teenage niece declared herself to be vegetarian, refusing any meat that was brought to the table, it was disastrous for Mira, whose entire oeuvre seemed inspired by her butchery roots, and who hated nothing more than someone who did not eat her food. I watched her prepare a dish for my niece's next visit, asking her what was in it. She was so cagey about it, so unwilling to reveal its ingredients, that I dubbed the dish Potato Surprise, a label with a punchline. The surprise, I wrote, was that some of the potatoes were actually bits of chicken masquerading as vegetables. I had made it up, of course, but the story became retold as fact, with Mira laughing whenever it was repeated, as if she were hearing a priceless joke for the very first time.

* * *

In 2012, Mira contributed to a Jewish cookbook, *Cooking from the Heart*, sharing some of her recipes and anecdotes about food. She had not been very interested in cooking when she was young, and remembered making many culinary missteps in adulthood. After the war, when produce was still scarce, she went to shop at the local food market in Kežmarok, returning home with a bag filled with small fish to cook – only to learn that she had actually purchased bait instead.

Another time, she tried her hand at cooking liver, which was hard to come by. Remembering the way her mother prepared most meals – putting ingredients in a pot and letting them simmer on a low flame – she thought the liver could be prepared that way too. When it finally arrived at the dinner table, it was inedible: so tough, it could barely be cut into pieces.

But underlying her cooking there was a greater significance. Her kitchen grew more kosher as she got older, and she rarely deviated from traditional dishes on Shabbat. When she was interviewed for the cookbook, she explained how intertwined her cooking was with her practice of Judaism. 'My children and grandchildren love to come on Friday nights. To me, it is a gathering of family; we are together.' In the same breath, Mira also recognised that it was very easy for Jewish people to become assimilated in Australia, losing sight of the importance of their religion in the process. She said, 'If you don't keep up the Jewishness, assimilation grows. Having been during the war and knowing what to be Jewish means, to turn the other way is very easy and often done here. I am hoping that my children and grandchildren are going to continue [in Judaism] and that they enjoy it. [On Friday nights,] it is important that they are together, that all the grandchildren know each other, that they talk – that [they know] they are family. Whatever I can do to contribute to that, I do. If it is because of the cooking [that they feel Jewish], so be it. That is my way.'

Seven

Mira's first real experience of antisemitism occurred when she was eleven. In her school class of thirty, there was a mix of Jewish and non-Jewish students, and the two groups mingled easily. One of her good friends was a non-Jewish girl whose lunches were an endless source of fascination. Instead of the sweet challah bread that Mira brought, her classmate's meal consisted of dark bread which her mother sometimes topped with sugar, and Mira would eagerly swap with her.

But it was never good to go to that friend's house, where conditions were poor and her domineering father was said to be violent – unhappy that his wife had borne three strong daughters and one weak son. His own children shook with fear when he approached them. He also belonged to the Hlinka Guard, the militia established by the pro-Nazi Slovak People's Party in 1938. One day, Mira's friend announced that her father did not like or trust the Jews. The words felt like a short, sharp sting that left an impression behind, like the tiny scar of an injection that you only notice when you catch sight of it in a mirror.

By then, the Blumenstocks had learned what happened when Hitler invaded Austria in March 1938, making it part of the German Reich. Jews were being persecuted there, but although it was a country not so geographically remote, it seemed like a world apart. 'When we heard that Hitler had gone in and what happened to the Jews there, we didn't believe it,' Mira said. 'It sounded like propaganda. We thought: *We live in the twentieth century.* And we knew the Germans to be very correct, to do things that were incredible … What we didn't know was that they would do something that was so incredible – something that so defied credibility – that people still don't believe it to this day.'

In March 1939, Hitler wanted to break apart Czechoslovakia, and the Slovak State was born. To Mira and her family, theirs had always been a democratic country until recently; the danger they'd heard about in faint whispers seemed very far away. That must have been true for others in their community as well. The town's rabbi was a revered man who rejected the tenets of Zionism: he did not believe that Jewish people should emigrate to Palestine until the Messiah came. Around a dozen Jewish young men had managed to leave together on a boat bound for the Holy Land, making *aliyah* – the emigration of Jews to the Land of Israel. But on the next Sabbath, my mother remembered the rabbi standing on his pulpit at synagogue and decrying their passage. He told the congregants that the men would no longer have a place in his *shule* – his synagogue – and neither would their families, if they chose to remain abroad. And so the parents did the unthinkable, given the course of history: they summoned their sons home.

Mira remembered German soldiers passing through the town in late August 1939, on their way to occupy Poland. No one could see what lay just days ahead: the leader of the Nazi Party, Adolf Hitler, would invade Poland on 1 September, with Britain and France declaring war on Germany two days later. It would mark the start of World War II.

When she and Dolfie stood by the side of the road watching as the soldiers marched through their town, Mira felt more than unsettled. She was so thrown by the sight that she started to laugh. Hysterical, uncontrollable laughter. 'Maybe it was fear,' she said later. 'It was very scary to see all those soldiers with their guns and looking very stern, so many of them.' She never forgot Dolfie's reaction when she started laughing; he gave her one quick slap across her face. She knew why he had done so: it was the only thing that would stop her hysterics immediately. Still, it was so very unusual. Dolfie had never physically disciplined any of his children, leaving Genya to dole out punishments. With their mother in charge, the worst that had ever happened was when Yanchi was struck with a tea towel for stealing the neighbour's apples, and he had hidden a soft pillow underneath his trousers so as to not feel the light blows she administered. The family had joked about it. This was so very, very different and disturbing.

Some of the soldiers fell out of the procession to rest, sitting on the pavement in front of the Blumenstocks' house. Dolfie still remembered what it was like to be in the army, and he sympathised with these uniformed men. He asked Genya to boil some water and cut some loaves, and soon she was offering the men cups of coffee and buttered bread.

They thanked her politely. And although the family had not yet learned how dangerous the German soldiers could be – these were not SS officers but the Wehrmacht, the German armed forces – they soon discovered something else: war was upon them.

* * *

The teachings of Hitler, who laid out his beliefs in his political manifesto *Mein Kampf*, had gripped Germany. Nazis promoted the idea that the German people were members of a superior 'Aryan race'. Jews, their most despised targets, were considered *Untermenschen*, or sub-human. But they were not the only ones the Nazis persecuted. Also included in their sights – because of their so-called racial or biological inferiority – were people of colour, Sinti and Roma (then called 'gypsies'), homosexuals and those with disabilities. Still, the Nazis were the most effective propagandists when declaring their hatred of Jews, and they had been broadcasting this message for some time – through theatre, films, books, newspapers, radio and whatever means they could. Jews were routinely depicted in posters as hook-nosed, diseased, insane, money-hungry.

On *Kristallnacht* – the Night of Broken Glass – in November 1938, thousands of Jewish businesses, synagogues and homes were subjected to wanton destruction and vandalism in Germany, Austria and the Sudetenland. Synagogues were burned, while firefighters and the public stood watching. But it was more brutal than that; Jews were killed and beaten; women raped. After it was over, it was the Jews who had to pay: the Nazi regime introduced a one-billion Reichsmark atonement tax, and used the event to enact anti-Jewish laws. The SS Gestapo arrested more than thirty thousand Jewish men. Most of them would end up in concentration camps.

For Mira, the situation in her town changed dramatically once the war broke out. When she was young, there was no rift between Jews and non-Jews, and the townspeople often spoke about the local Catholic priest and Jewish rabbi named Mordekhai Strasser, who were such good friends that they regularly went for walks together in the cabbage fields behind the parish garden. When the priest died of old age, the rabbi wrote a sermon about him that was read on Saturday in the synagogue and again on Sunday in the church. And not long before, when Tomáš Garrigue Masaryk had been President of Czechoslovakia – a position he held for seventeen years, until late 1935 – Dolfie would say how blessed they were to be under his leadership, in a country where it seemed like there was no antisemitism, and Jews felt free to observe their religion. Not that it had been much of an issue in Spišská Stará Ves, where the local Jewish men largely roamed the streets without yarmulkes (skullcaps), and nothing in their clothing or appearance set them visibly apart from the rest of the community.

By September 1940, when Mira was thirteen, an edict had been issued and she, as a Jew, was not allowed to attend her school anymore. It was a shock to her, and she felt as though everything had changed from one day to the next. Last week, she had played with her non-Jewish schoolfriend. This week, when Mira passed her on the street, her friend looked down at the ground, ignoring her.

Now, Jewish families had to improvise. They were not sure how long the war would last or when their children could return to public classrooms. To continue their children's education, they hired a teacher from the larger city of Bratislava, and the students were divided into older and younger groups. Mr Steiner, the teacher, was a likeable man who understood how to make the lessons interesting and fun. The Blumenstocks got to know him well, since he rented a room in their house. At the end of the year, an inspector was brought in to test each child in various subjects, awarding them a certificate if they passed – an acknowledgement that they were entitled to move up a grade. It was an arrangement that stayed in place until 1942.

Many vestiges of their old lives slipped away for the children, but one thing remained for Yanchi. He was like a firefly on the soccer field, moving so quickly that it became dizzying to follow him. He had been a child who was never without a ball, and it had been his siblings' game to try to take it from him. But his feet were faster than anyone's, his movements more fluid. It was impossible.

Before the war, the coach of the local team visited the Blumenstock home to ask if Yanchi could fill in as goalkeeper for a kid who was sick. Yanchi had only ever played with the Jewish soccer team, but since the locals all knew each other, his father agreed. He was so skilled that they kept him on as a permanent team member.

He continued playing even when the war was in its infancy, and one season the team drew a game in another town. Dolfie did not see how it was possible for Yanchi to join them. In Spišská Stará Ves, everyone knew his son, and no harm would befall him. But in a foreign town, if they got wind of the fact that he was Jewish … anything could happen. If antisemitism had been only a faint undercurrent before the war, now the family could feel it everywhere. Still, the coach was convincing. 'Mr Blumenstock, I vouch with my life that nothing will happen to your son. If we don't have Yanchi, we will lose: it's as simple as that. If we want to win, he has to be there.' After much persuasion, Dolfie agreed, and the team won. But what Mira remembered best was how everyone loved Yanchi. 'He was such a *chevreman*,' she said, using a term that described him as one of the guys, a people person.

Meanwhile, Olga had recently wed – on 29 May 1939 – at the age of twenty-three. Her husband was not her first love. Several years before the war began, she had gone on a holiday to Poland to visit some relatives. There she met a young man, and they were instantly smitten. Olga was quiet, like her mother, but I imagine he, as the eldest child in a family of five, made her laugh and feel more carefree than she usually did. She was convinced that her parents would adore him; they had always assured their children that they would never talk them out of marriage if it was to someone their child loved. So when Olga returned to her home town, her young man came to visit her.

For some reason – Mira never knew what it was – Dolfie disliked him. He claimed that this suitor was not observant enough, even though they themselves were not so *frum*; Dolfie was not someone who wore a *shtreimel*, a large fur hat, like some of the Hasidic men in other towns. Genya never went to synagogue unless it was a High Holy Day. And Heshek and

Shani, who each lived out of home, did no more than observe the main Jewish festivals. This niggled at Dolfie, who always made his sons put on their tefillin, the small black boxes that contain scrolls of parchment inscribed with Torah verses, to say their morning prayers whenever there was an opportunity. Perhaps this was at the heart of why Dolfie held firm in his belief that Olga's choice was a poor one.

The next time Olga's paramour paid a visit, Dolfie was determined to keep them apart. 'He said to my sister, "You go in the house, and don't leave,"' said Mira. 'I was told to stay with her. My father said, "If the boy wants to come to see her, don't let him in."'

Genya did not intervene, but both girls knew their mother would never contradict her husband.

'It's a sad, sad story,' Mira said, 'because unfortunately my sister's hope of love was completely demolished. She never married anyone she loved.'

That was Mira's take, anyway. Olga went on to marry Arnošt Glückstahl, a man ten years her senior, of whom twelve-year-old Mira did not form a strong impression; years later, she struggled to remember his name. But for Olga, marriage was important, perhaps more than ever; she wanted her freedom. 'Because what could a girl do at that time if she wanted to be independent?' Mira mused. 'She knew how to sew, but in our town how much could she earn doing that?'

I would later wonder if Mira's assessment was too harsh. In one photo of Olga and Arnošt, he stands behind her, holding her. He looks upon her with a tender gaze that suggests he has something precious in his grasp. Meanwhile, Olga is smiling widely. She is the one who looks strong in this photo; it is as if he holds her in order to steady himself. Apart from his receding hairline, they do not look so mismatched.

Ironically, Olga never left her parents' home; the newlyweds took up residence in one of the bedrooms at the Blumenstock house. She and Arnošt had a vision for their future: they planned to emigrate to Palestine, at Dolfie's urging. Seeing the increasing hardships that Jews endured, Dolfie sought to get the family out of the country. Finally, in 1940, he managed to secure two tickets on a ship bound for Palestine, and gave these to Olga and Arnošt. It had cost him a great deal of money, but the voyage was cancelled at the last minute. Dolfie not only lost the price of the tickets; his ability to protect his family was being challenged daily, from moment to moment.

It was not the only time Dolfie had tried to arrange safe passage from Europe for those in his care; he had long been trying to obtain travelling papers and sponsorship through relatives in America. He was a man of action and careful thought, so likely these steps had been taken logically, purposefully. But there was another trait that ran through the family, seldom acknowledged: premonition. Mira often felt it, creeping under her skin like a virus. Perhaps Dolfie felt it too.

* * *

When I was growing up, my mother relied strongly on her intuition. 'I have a bad feeling,' she would say, and her face would darken. Usually this involved circuitous arrangements; she did not like it when things were overly complicated or not straightforward. But she also did not believe in tempting fate in any way: she did not want anyone in her family to catch a plane over the Sabbath, and as a child I was never allowed to hold my birthday party before its actual date.

Many old Eastern European superstitions found their way into my childhood. Mira refused to return home if she had forgotten something after she had just left, likely drawing from the Russian superstition which held that doing so would set the day off in the wrong direction, begging for misfortune. She did not let her daughters sit at the corner of a table before they were married (lest it ruin their chances of betrothal for seven years) and would also stop someone from stepping over another person's legs (in case it stopped them growing). If I said something foreboding to my mother, such as 'I hope I don't catch a cold,' she would quickly make a sound of spitting – 'Peh, peh, peh' – which was supposedly a way to stop the terrible thing from occurring. If I put on a becoming outfit, she would immediately reach for something red to put on me, harking back to olden times when red strings were worn around wrists as talismans to ward off the evil eye. As a child, I had many pairs of red underwear.

Consequently, I grew up doing everything I could to avoid misfortune. I did not step on pavement cracks, I did not walk underneath ladders. At the same time, I made wishes whenever possible: on first stars in the sky, on sneezes, when I threw coins into lakes, when an eyelash skittered across my cheek. I made those wishes to counteract anything that might go wrong, because I had a deep-seated fear that *everything* might go wrong.

With few exceptions, Jewish people are not supposed to believe in superstitions, but Mira certainly did not want to invoke bad luck in any way. Perhaps when you have witnessed the unluckiest of times, adhering to superstitions is a kind of insurance: it demonstrates the belief that one's fortune can always be turned around.

Eight

The Blumenstocks' store continued to stay open, although the sign that once hung above the door – A. BLUMENSTOCK – had been changed. It now read: J. SCHOLCZ. The majority of Jewish people had their properties and businesses confiscated under the *Land Reform Act* of February 1940, whereby Jewish-owned land would pass to the State Land Office. The idea was presented as social policy – making the 'wealthy' Jews surrender property to their 'poor' non-Jewish counterparts – but in reality it was just another way to strip Jewish people of their status and their stronghold.

This 'forced aryanisation' had a loophole of sorts. Some Jews who owned businesses were able to make a deal with a Christian candidate, known as an *arizátor*, offering them at least 51 per cent of the business for no return. This meant that Jews could still retain a portion of their businesses, albeit less than half. Still, it was not easy for Jewish people to make these arrangements, or find someone they could trust.

Dolfie had a head start, having heard that these laws would be passed. As one of the unofficial communal leaders for the Jewish people in his town, he had inner dealings with the gendarmerie, a branch of the military that policed civilians, and he paid them handsomely for inside information. At that time, Heshek – who was working in Kežmarok – had a sympathetic boss, a non-Jewish man who owned a wholesale material store. When the two discussed the problem, Heshek's boss mentioned his brother, a barber with a wife and two children, who might be able to help. A deal was struck.

This was how the majority of the Blumenstocks' store came to be owned by Mr Julius Scholcz – a Sudeten German – with Dolfie remaining as a silent partner of sorts; Scholcz's background in hairdressing had not prepared him to run a shop, so he needed the assistance of Dolfie and his family. It proved to be a mutually beneficial arrangement, with Mr Scholcz trying not to take advantage of the situation, and Dolfie getting more than he was supposed to in his new position.

Mira grew friendly with Scholcz's two children – Hilda, his daughter, who was two years older than her, and Julla, his son, one year her junior. Mira, ever the reliable worker, stood by their side in the store, demonstrating the processes and dealing with the customers she had known for so long. Beyond the functional role that the Scholcz family played, they also offered a very slight semblance of normality. Julius's wife, Anna, was a kind woman, and Mira was always welcome in her home. The youngsters would beg her to tell them a story, since she had an almost encyclopaedic memory for books she had read and films she had seen long ago. She would describe them in evocative detail, and the children would sit there rapt. Mira, not yet fourteen, was still in thrall of a make-believe story that could momentarily transport her far, far away.

But conditions grew progressively worse for many Jewish people. From October 1939, Germans had begun establishing ghettoes; a year later, there was one in the Polish city of Warsaw, which also had the largest Jewish community in Europe. There, Jews were forced into horrendous living conditions, with extreme overcrowding, lack of hygiene and minimal rations, leading many to die of disease and hunger.

In the Slovak State, too, the atmosphere was growing darker. In September 1941, anyone who was Jewish – or even half-Jewish – was ordered to wear articles on their clothing signifying so, usually a Star of David on their coats. Ostensibly these emblems identified Jews. Psychologically, they were intended to mark Jewish people as different and inferior, to isolate and dehumanise them. Mira remembers that 'it was very oppressive. You knew you were not allowed to do anything – go to the same places as before, or talk to your old schoolfriends. You did not mix with anyone other than Jewish people, and there was always this fear of what was going to come next.'

Other edicts were issued. Jews had to surrender their passports. Slovak officials continued to confiscate Jewish private property – not just real estate, but bank accounts and household items. So much had to be given up, even the seemingly trivial, including radio sets, fishing equipment, cameras, gramophone records and telescopes. Jews could not own cars. They could not enter any public parks.

Mira remembered the day when the Hlinka Guard raided her house. Without warning, these men in military uniform stomped through her home with disdain and disregard for its inhabitants. Anything that was of value was immediately seized: ornate silver candlesticks used for the Sabbath blessings, jewellery, a radio, chandeliers, bedside lamps – 'everything that was more than just bare necessities,' recalled Mira. They opened each drawer of the bureaus; 'they really plundered everything'.

Dolfie stood by watching silently, until the guards opened a cupboard and discovered the brand-new winter coat he had bought his wife as a gift only a month earlier. 'I remember that the coat was the pride of my father, because after working so hard for many, many years, he could finally afford to buy her a nice coat.' He had remained quiet when the other items were carted away, but when they tried to take the coat, he spoke up. 'No!' he shouted. 'You can take everything else but you will not be taking this away! This coat stays with my wife!' It was her father's demeanour that Mira never forgot. 'We could not believe it, because my father was not a man who would get angry or scream. He was very self-controlled.' But in this instance, his anger blazed. 'We were very proud of him, because they left without taking the coat.'

* * *

I thought about that coat and what it represented when I saw the movie *Woman in Gold*, right after Mira's cancer diagnosis. In it, Helen Mirren plays Maria Altmann, a Jewish woman from Austria whose family was wealthy and cultured, and whose aunt was famously portrayed in artist Gustav Klimt's painting, *Portrait of Adele Bloch-Bauer I*. After that artwork was seized by the Nazis, it ended up in Vienna's Belvedere Palace and was renowned as 'Austria's *Mona Lisa*'. Altmann embarked on a legal battle with the Austrian government to reclaim it, additionally demanding that they publicly admit the country's Jewish citizens had been tragically robbed of so much in the past.

My mother did not see any Holocaust movies or read any Holocaust literature as a rule; it was too upsetting, and she would suffer waves of nightmares for days afterwards. But when I recounted the details of this film to her, she surprised me by saying she would like to see it. As a journalist, I was invited to private screenings, and so we went to view it in a small theatrette together with other members of the media. I remember having the urge to stand up and tell the audience that my mother had lived through the Holocaust; I wanted everyone to know that there was a real-life survivor among them, someone as worthy of their admiration as Maria Altmann.

Mira was eighty-eight, but still relatively nimble. When we walked into the theatre, I noted how diminutive she was, but how proudly erect she stood. Despite the fact that it was my second time watching the movie, I cried. Mira did not. She sat there silently, even though some of the scenes echoed ones from her own life. When the Altmann home is stormed, the family watch helplessly as their rooms are upended and valuables are stolen.

After the lights went up, we spoke about the portions of the movie with which Mira identified, such as when Mirren, as Altmann, says, 'I have to do what I can to keep these memories alive because people forget, you see – especially the young.' But the scene that bothered Mira most was when a Viennese man berated Altmann for continuing to pursue her case, questioning why she couldn't move on. 'Why does everything have to be about the Holocaust for you people?' he asked. My mother thought about this, about how the world is so anxious to deny the terrors of the past, or at least keep them firmly locked into the category of ancient history. Mira explained it this way to me: 'When you imagine yourself in Maria Altmann's shoes, it's very sad … you see how terrifying it was at the beginning of the war, when the world felt so unsafe. But for me, I lived it.'

What she was trying to say was that some things can't be forgotten, or swept away. Mira might have managed to keep the past from wrapping its tentacles around her throat, but it was a part of her, a small beating heart that remained fixed in its own immovable spot.

Nine

When the transports started in Slovakia in March 1942, Mira was one month shy of fifteen. Heshek was living away and working, while Shani had been drafted into the Sixth Slovak Brigade, the Šiesty prápor. This was an army unit created for Jews – and Sinti and Roma – who were not allowed to report for military service. Instead, they undertook forced labour, and mainly did work such as digging soil and paving roads. The only Blumenstock 'children' left in the family home were Mira, Yanchi and Olga, along with Olga's husband, Arnošt.

An announcement was made in Spišská Stará Ves's centre: first by a town drummer, and later by large posters affixed to the walls. Initially, young, unmarried Jewish women were called up, ordered to report at a specified location. The purpose was unclear, other than they knew they were being sent away 'to work'. People were confused: what kind of work would these young girls be able to do, and why were they the first to go? Mira was exempt, thanks to the paperwork stating that she was needed by Julius Scholcz in the family's old store, and so she did not join the dozens of girls from the district – among them many teenagers – who boarded that first train from Poprad.

Mira remembered that not long afterwards, some of the men were summoned to report to central locations. It was their understanding that they would go to a labour camp where conditions were good, returning when their work was done. Mira's uncle Samuel was eligible, as was her brother-in-law, Arnošt.

Suddenly there were preparations to be made, and perhaps that activity distracted them from focusing on what might lie ahead. Everyone was given a list of items that they could bring, each of which had a specified size and weight range. The women busied themselves cooking food: they dried out bread to make crusts that would last longer, and added small packets of roux – a mixture of flour, butter and salt that could be combined with water or milk to form a soup.

Dolfie urged Arnošt to disobey the order, convincing Olga and her husband to hide at their *arizátor* Mr Scholcz's house, where they could be secreted away safely. The couple did so for a short time, but Arnošt came to think this was a bad idea; he was not afraid of work, he said. He urged his wife to go too, as he did not want to be separated from her. Ultimately, they presented themselves for the transports when the orders came.

Olga must have felt somewhat secure in her decision; the war had been going for two and a half years already, and while some Jews were living in terrible and oppressive conditions, no one had heard of anything worse than that. And she was young, fit and compliant – surely factors in her favour. Before her departure, Dolfie made his eldest daughter memorise an address in Poland. His connection with the partisans – the resistance fighters – had been well established by then, and he thought there was a chance that Olga could still be smuggled out to Hungary, which the Germans had yet to occupy. If she sent a letter to that address, a partisan would be able to retrieve it and bring it to the Blumenstocks.

Sure enough, after some time, a letter arrived. Dolfie could tell it had been heavily censored; it did not sound like his daughter at all. Still, it was in her handwriting, written in German, and the first part reassured him. 'We have arrived safely,' she wrote.

Later, a second letter arrived from Olga, this one far more ominous. 'Everything is all right here, but do everything that you can not to visit me.' The words were buried amid other details, so their import was not immediately apparent. But when Dolfie read it, a jolt of fear took hold in him so strongly and fiercely that he could never thereafter shake it. He replayed the words in his head every day, trying to make them sound less jarring, less haunting. He never managed to do so.

* * *

After Olga had been deported, Dolfie prayed every morning and night that he would see her again. It was impossible to think otherwise. He could easily imagine his eldest daughter before him: Olga, who looked so similar to Mira with the same ready smile, but who was often so pensive and introspective.

Still, he did not want to be one of those men who denied the possibility of terrible things. He hoped he would see Olga one day, but deep down he knew that he might not. He did not relay this terrible thought to Genya or anyone else. He let it sit lodged in his belly, where it grew more gangrenous by the day. He would not allow anything bad to happen to the family members who were still under his roof. 'At all costs, we have to avoid being taken away,' he told them. And he started putting plans in place.

* * *

Mira would never learn precisely what had happened to Olga. When the very first lot of deported women boarded the train in Slovakia on 25 March, they were unaware of what lay ahead and tried to stay optimistic. Some of the girls sang songs in Slovak and Hebrew as they attempted to keep their fear at bay. Did the same thing happen when Olga left, not long afterwards? She was initially allowed to send those censored letters, which was a ruse devised by the SS: if families back home were lulled into a sense of security about the camps, they would not be so reluctant to go when rounded up themselves. Across the country, other families had received similar postcards which sounded equally scripted. 'Everything is fine! We have plenty to eat! Hope to see you soon!' Some households would receive those cards for months to come, believing on that basis that their loved ones were still alive. They were unaware that their daughters had been forced to write several letters at once, dating them months apart.

One survivor told Mira that she had met Olga, and believed her to have been part of a group plotting their escape, not wanting to leave their fate in the hands of the Nazis. They were never able to carry out their plan; the next day, the women were again put on trucks and taken away.

A record of Jews from Slovakia who were deported indicates that Olga was taken to Izbica Ghetto, in occupied Poland, which acted as a transit camp. There, she would have been housed in vastly overcrowded conditions in wooden barracks, or made to sleep outdoors; it was during this period that she likely sent her postcards home. She also would have witnessed the random acts of cruelty that took place. Perhaps she died of typhus, as so many did there. The Jews who managed to stay put until November 1942 were ultimately massacred. But most were transported beforehand, either to Bełżec or Sobibor death camps.

Olga would have met a similar end in each camp. On the premise that she needed to be 'disinfected', she would have undressed and entered a chamber. Her hair would have been shorn, because the Nazis could make a profit selling bales of women's hair, to be repurposed into items such as fabric rolls. Even when the chamber was full, more prisoners would have been forced in – the guards beating them with either clubs or whips to ensure they crammed into the space. Gas would then flood the building, slowly killing her and everyone else. Finally, Olga's body would be burned, but not before any metal dental work was pulled from her mouth and jewellery removed.

Neither Olga nor her husband, Arnošt, was ever seen again. Because the records were so incomplete, not even the date of her death was known. Whenever Mira spoke about her only sister, she wept: not just for the shortness of twenty-six-year-old Olga's life, but for the sadness in it too.

* * *

Like Mira, I knew what it meant to have an older sister, for I have two: Lilianne is twelve years older than me, Jeannette fifteen. Both infused my childhood with a pinch of magic. Lilianne taught me how to draw realistic eyes, introduced me to the work of Renoir and Kandinsky at the National Gallery of Victoria's Modern Masters exhibition and took me ice-skating at the St. Moritz rink with the warning that I should always curl my hand into a fist if I fell so that no one would accidentally slice off my fingers with the blades of their skates. Jeannette invented lively games for my birthday parties and took me to the St Kilda Botanical Gardens, where a grassy mound became an island on which I was shipwrecked and my stories of fairies and witches could be indulged.

On weekend afternoons, when my sisters had gone out, I would quietly creep into their bedrooms, hoping to discover the mysteries of young women through their possessions, a snooping archaeologist studying teen artefacts of the 1970s. Jeannette had small tubs of cream on her bureau, a collection of short, baby-doll nighties and a teased-up wig which sat perched atop a Styrofoam head. Lilianne owned a blue chenille bedspread with fringing along the bottom, two wooden figures of Adam and Eve that fit together erotically, and a framed print of the poem 'Desiderata'.

By the time I was ten, both of them had moved out of home, and their absence left me with mixed emotions. I would no longer be able to rummage in Lilianne's desk drawer for illicit scribblings, or sneak into Jeannette's room when it was dark to watch *The Don Lane Show* on a tiny black and white television.

On the other hand, I had my pick of their coveted bedrooms; Lilianne's was dominated by a stained-glass window, a lush melange of red roses and leaves, while Jeannette's was larger and more substantial, a grown-up's boudoir.

But what I did not know then, when all the rooms were first emptied of their movements, their sounds, their smells of patchouli and moisturiser, was how the notion of sisterhood would be imprinted on me. How they would forever be the witnesses of my past, co-treasurers of our shared memories. How their mannerisms would always be so familiar to me that even if I caught a gesture from a distance – a hand fluttering, for instance – I would always know it was them. There might be times in the future when they would get to me – they could bring tears of both happiness and frustration to my eyes – but that was only because of the claim they had on me. They were part of me, linked by blood and history and all the qualities that our parents had invested us with.

My mother never told me any of this, and I think that was because she did not know what a sister could become. She was fifteen when Olga left, and that is too young to know that the sister who is still mysterious and distant might eventually be the person who makes you feel that you are not so alone in the world. I do not remember my mother ever telling me that I should keep my sisters' secrets close, and commit the sounds of their laughter to memory. She never told me they would one day clear road bumps and debris from my path; she never mentioned that it was important not to break my connection with them because it had the potential to be stronger than anything else. She never told me these things, because she never found out herself.

Ten

The transport that took place in the middle of 1942 was designed to scoop up the remaining Jewish families from Spišská Stará Ves and neighbouring districts. Less than a dozen families – including the Blumenstocks – were exempted. Around 180 people had to gather at the synagogue just a few doors down from Mira's home. Why did so many people acquiesce, rather than hide? Some did hide, of course. But there were serious consequences for those who disobeyed. And many people still believed that they were going to some kind of labour camp, which would be harsh, but survivable. It was impossible to look around at all those gathered in the synagogue – young parents, babies, the elderly – and think that they might not return.

Among them was Mira's eighty-year-old grandmother Chava, sickly with a heart condition. There too were her thirty-four-year-old aunt Klara – Samuel's wife – and their son, her seven-year-old cousin Imrich. Mira walked to the *shule* to bid them farewell, but was shocked when she crossed the entrance and saw that it was flanked by half-a-dozen uniformed guards with rifles. She knew those guards personally; the whole village knew each other. Inside she saw a throng of people, some able to rest on the synagogue's benches and chairs but many of the adults sitting on the hard, wooden floor, with their small bundles of belongings next to them. Her parents were not with her – they would come separately – so she faced the situation alone. There were people crying uncontrollably. Children were whining, begging to go outdoors. Mira saw some of her friends – close friends, whom she had once known intimately – but when she caught their eye, they turned and huddled in their group, pretending not to have noticed her. She knew why: she was one of the lucky ones, allowed to stay behind.

She could hardly believe this was the house of prayer she had known so well for many years, an institution in her community for over a century, now a jail. She had run up and down its aisles as a young child, hiding behind her father's *tallit*, his prayer shawl. She had stood quietly by her mother's side when she was older, holding a *machzor*, a prayer book, in her hands. Amid this scene, it was incongruous to catch sight of the ornate *Aron Kodesh*, the ark that held the Torah scrolls, itself inscribed with holy scripture. She could not remember what those Hebrew words meant, but she thought it was this: *Be aware before whom you stand.*

In the crowd she found her grandmother, sitting on a bench and holding Imrich in her arms. She was not crying. But when Mira saw the sad, frightened expression on Chava's face, she had a feeling in her own heart that she would later describe as a 'deep hurt'. Suddenly, she couldn't breathe. She couldn't wait to step outside and inhale fresh air again. 'I was scared of the brutality of the whole thing.'

The worst was seeing the rabbi. Mira did not recognise him at first, despite knowing him her whole life. His *payot*, or sidelocks, had been shorn, along with his long beard and hair. She had never seen someone so pale – he was 'snow white' – but there was something more disturbing than that. 'His eyes were burning out. And to look at him – my God. He looked terrible, terrible: like a ghost.' He had once ordered a dozen local boys to return from Palestine. Perhaps at last he understood what fate awaited them.

Before she left, Mira embraced her grandmother. She was not wondering when she would next see her; that did not really cross her mind. In those airless months, the future was impossible to contemplate. But she said, 'Babush, I hope everything will be all right. You will be okay there.' Her grandmother looked at her, too stunned and deflated to pretend anymore. She did not say a word. She just shook her head.

The next morning, Mira heard noise in the road outside. She ran to the footpath just in time to see the truck that was taking her grandmother away.

She would never see any of those people who had sat in the synagogue again.

* * *

I don't remember the first time my parents took me to Elwood *shule*, the synagogue located a three-minute walk from my childhood home. It had always been a fixture in my life, as familiar to me as my own house. When I was little, *shule* was a place to play and hide: under creaky seats, in the cloakroom and also in the little anteroom you had to walk through to get to the ladies'. There, heavyset women didn't like you sitting on the floor with a friend, blocking their way so they were forced to climb over your stockinged legs. The *shule* smelled of the crinkly pages of old *siddurs* mixed with the aged wood of the benches. I always made sure to visit the designated lolly man. He would reach into the seat of his chair – it flipped open like a magic box to store prayer books – and hand over three boiled sweets if you said hello nicely.

As I got older, I would sit in the upper gallery by my mother's side – men and women were seated separately – and share her prayer book. My lips moved with hers as the service progressed, and if I paused for too long she would elbow me and point to the place we were up to in the service. Her prayer books had German translations, so I was not sure what the Hebrew words meant, but it did not matter to my mother. She wanted to hear the Hebrew words read aloud, to invest in me the feeling they imbued.

From that vantage point, we could watch the men below, and in the days when the *shule* overflowed on High Holy Days, we looked out onto a sea of black suits and white prayer shawls, each punctuated with dark hats or yarmulkes that sat atop the men's heads. They would *shockel*, swaying from the waist in that rhythmic back-and-forth movement seen in all Orthodox synagogues, moving in time with the beat of the prayers. It was hypnotic, and because they said the Hebrew words so quickly, listening to them from afar was like hearing an accordant vibration. My mother would often close her eyes to concentrate better. When it came time for the *Birkat Kohanim* – the Priestly Blessing – I knew that I wasn't meant to stare at the men, thereby allowing them to properly bless the whole congregation without distraction. Still, I would always be mesmerised by this strange benediction, in which they would cover their heads with their prayer shawls, looking like bobbing white ghosts, while chanting the words of the blessing.

Once, I asked Mira, 'Why do you like to go to *shule* so often?' She occasionally went on a Saturday morning for Shabbat, and attended during festivals. She laughed, and said she had started going in earnest once she'd had four children; she needed to get out of the house, and services offered the best opportunity.

But I knew there was something more that I could not see. When she prayed in synagogue, she was transported to a place that brought tears to her eyes. I knew it brought her solace, too. Neither of us spoke fluent Hebrew, but when we heard a word we knew among the prayers, it rose above the rest and so took on gravitas: *Baruch* (blessed), *Chayim* (life), *Eloheinu* (our God). I would listen to these guttural sounds and feel them viscerally in my chest; they felt primal and deeply rooted. They were foreign and familiar at the same time. And they were words of connection: I knew that my grandparents and great-grandparents would have uttered these words themselves, in synagogues not unlike my own. For my mother, her own attachment to them was being formed again and again. It was in this place that she could feel her ancestors, and perhaps even hear them. She could no longer see them, but in synagogue they could leap from her memory and come closer to her.

Eleven

By the end of 1942 there were only eight Jewish families left in Spišská Stará Ves, including the Blumenstocks and their two youngest children. They kept themselves occupied with their daily affairs, becoming more self-sufficient than ever. Genya no longer had the help of a maid, since a Slovak person was not allowed to work for a Jew. There was no kosher meat to be had – the *shochet*, or ritual slaughterer, had been taken on the last transport – but the family still managed to obtain meat for the High Holy Days, clandestinely arranging for a *shochet* to come from two towns over. Mira questioned his experience; he looked young, and set about killing a chicken in a dark shed at the rear of their house. He wasn't very effective, and Genya had to help him finish the task.

But they always found a way to remember who they were. For Passover, they went to another town where one Jewish household owned a large oven. All eight families from Spišská Stará Ves baked their matzos, or unleavened bread, there. Dolfie no longer owned a radio – it had been confiscated – but he tried to keep abreast of the news, mainly through the intel of Heshek, who had an elevated status through his job, allowing him to move from place to place as a travelling salesman.

There was not much they could do for entertainment; there was an 8 p.m. curfew, and Jews were now forbidden from entering many local haunts. Gone were the days when WIZO, the Women's International Zionist Organization, was able to host a ball in the town's three-room hotel. In the early evening, they mainly played cards, gathering with the other remaining families. Although they did not socialise with anyone non-Jewish in their town, there were some neighbours who did not shun them on account of their religion. They would still come into the store and engage in friendly chatter; likewise, the Blumenstocks were also welcome in their retail premises. Several would go even further, offering shelter or help to the Jews they knew, thereby putting themselves in danger. But many more were bystanders, or even worse: Mira's cousin Kurt recalled people standing in the street in Kežmarok and calling out, 'Have a nice sleigh ride' to the Jews who were being carted off in trucks, destination unknown.

* * *

He might have had an outwardly calm and quiet demeanour, but Dolfie Blumenstock was never someone who would unquestioningly follow rules. Mira sometimes heard the whispered conversations her father conducted in his store with the partisans, whose underground network was secretly fighting the inner workings of Nazi Germany and its collaborators. Some of them were engaged in sabotage; others in guerilla warfare. Over the next year, Mira watched as her father and brother Heshek became instrumental in smuggling Jews out of the Bochnia and Warsaw ghettos. They enlisted the help of non-Jewish drivers to bring those fugitives into Spišská Stará Ves and Kežmarok, thereafter hiding them in homes, including the Blumenstocks' own, before sending them on to Budapest, Hungary. Not only was it safer there at that time, but the Jewish Agency helped fund the cause, and documents were forged so that new arrivals were issued with identity certificates which allowed them to stay.

Mira recalled up to eight people hiding in their house at a time, sometimes staying for several nights. This was an incredibly dangerous and risky endeavour, and none of the neighbours could find out. If many people came at once, the Blumenstocks would not have beds for them all, but always ensured their comfort. They would offer blankets and food, with Genya putting extra wood in the stove to keep the house warm. Those who arrived were generally in poor health, their thin bodies telling an unspoken story of suffering. Mira remembered the family nursing a woman who appeared in a sickly state with a high fever, unable to eat much. They kept her safe until she was well enough to move on.

Heshek would later estimate that several hundred Jews passed through his father's house. In the Jewish text known as the Talmud – a book of religious and theological laws – it says that whoever kills one life kills the world entire; whoever saves one life saves the world entire. In this way, perhaps many worlds were saved within Dolfie and Genya's humble home.

* * *

Dolfie never became complacent. As soon as he received Olga's card, he built a hiding place for his two youngest children in case of an emergency, creating a loft at the top of his barn, which could be entered through a small, square gap close to the ground. The inner wall had to be scaled by climbing steps made from little pieces of wood, and the opening was camouflaged with more wooden planks.

One day, business took Dolfie to the city of Kežmarok. While he was away, a contact at the gendarmerie arrived with information: the authorities were looking for Jews, and the Blumenstocks should hide immediately. Genya worried about what to do. It was nearly impossible for her to climb the loft; only her children could easily scramble up and down the makeshift steps. So she made a different arrangement. The family's *arizátor*, Mr Scholcz, was willing to help, and he agreed to bring food to the children daily while they were in hiding. Meanwhile, Genya walked to the next town of Matiašovce, where she knew a Jewish family that remained living there.

She began walking at night, heavy clouds looming overhead. Thunder boomed in the dark sky, and rain began falling heavily. The wild wind made each step slower. Finally she arrived at her destination, only to be told by the family that they too had received a notice; officials were coming for them in the morning. So Genya – exhausted, her clothes drenched – turned to go home again.

It was still the middle of the night when she stood underneath the loft, calling out quietly so as not to be heard by anyone who might be lurking nearby. 'Children, children.' Mira stirred, and at first Yanchi told her she was hearing things. It took him a moment to be convinced that it was his mother. When they realised she had returned, they proceeded to haul her up to the loft themselves. It was a mighty task. She was neither agile nor light, and so they pushed her from behind, certain they were covering her soft body in bruises.

There they stayed, in these tiny quarters, for over a week. But another problem arose: Mira was clearly allergic to the hay. Her face became increasingly puffy and swollen as the days wore on. Word was sent to Heshek, who devised another plan: he arranged for a truckload of ready-to-wear women's coats to be delivered to the Blumenstock (now Scholcz) shop at night, accompanied by a workman. As the workman started unpacking the coats, Heshek instructed him to leave a bundle behind. These were used to shield his family as they climbed into the bottom of the vehicle, covering themselves with the garments. Once safely concealed, they drove to Roza and Gerson Storch's family home in Kežmarok, where his uncle and aunt's papers exempted them and their son Kurt from deportation.

In the Storches' backyard, there was a woodshed with a hidden second floor. Logs were stored beneath, and a retractable ladder could be dropped from above. The Blumenstocks were not the only family in hiding there; they were joined by a young married couple and their newborn baby, and were reunited with Dolfie. During the day, Roza brought them all food and drink, and at night they would each take turns going into the house to wash themselves. The location could not have been worse: next to the Storches' home was a bowling club where the Germans would gather. From the woodshed, it was easy to hear them speaking.

After several days of hiding, they heard footsteps nearby. Everyone held their breath. They could clearly hear the voices of two German soldiers, searching the property for any Jews. The pair stood directly underneath the loft. No one dared move an inch; it took all Mira's will to refrain from shaking. She did not dare look at the baby, whose mewls could sometimes be piercing when awake. Even the smallest whimper, right now, would be audible. '*Sollen wir da oben mal nachschauen?*' one soldier asked the other. 'Should we have a look up there?' Mira could imagine the scene unfolding: the men would open the door and see seven of them huddled within. They would all be carted away immediately.

But the other soldier replied, 'Ach, leave me alone; you can see that no one is there.'

Within a few minutes, they were gone.

Mira forever marvelled at that incredible stroke of luck: the baby had slept through the entire thing. Still, the soldiers' arrival had highlighted how inadequate and unsafe their hiding space was. It was time to find refuge elsewhere.

Aunt Roza had another solution: her cleaning lady, a non-Jewish woman, agreed to hide the Blumenstocks for a few days until the immediate danger had passed. There was just one catch: she lived with her elderly father, who would not have been amenable to breaking the law, thus risking severe consequences. She could fit two families – seven people in all – in her large pantry, which had a lock on its door, but they would need to be extremely quiet so as not to disturb her father.

A day in this new hiding spot passed, then another. Sunday arrived. Their benefactor left to go to church. Suddenly, there was a loud rapping on the pantry door, followed by yelling. 'Where is the bloody key?' Fear flooded Mira, clouding her eyes, her throat, her thoughts. 'We were absolutely so frightened, because it was life and death,' she said. Soon it became clear what was happening: the old man wanted entry to the pantry. He was calling out for sausages and other foods. The seven of them had to endure his raucous shouts and door-rattling until his daughter arrived home.

At night, when her father was asleep, the woman led the two families to the house's lone bedroom, where bedding had been arranged in a row against the wall. Mira, the smallest, shared a bed with the cleaning lady. Occasionally, the old man wanted to use the bathroom, but – given his failing eyesight and unsteady gait – he could not walk there on his own. He had a signal for summoning his daughter: he would reach across his own bed to hers, tugging on her hair to wake her. One night, he pulled Mira's hair by mistake. Mira woke up in fear, but knew better than to make a sound. Instead, she grabbed the daughter's hand, placing it on her head as well to indicate what had happened. Luckily, the woman reacted quickly, reassuring her father in the dark that she was taking him to the toilet. 'At the time, every minute felt really very dangerous,' said Mira.

After a week, they returned home. By now, the Germans had cleared the area. Dolfie had a relationship with a priest who, for a fee, was willing to oversee conversions. Yanchi became Greek Orthodox, even though there was no Greek Orthodox church in Spišská Stará Ves. This worked to his advantage since the nearest church was twelve miles away. It helped explain why Yanchi could not attend services every

Sunday. At the same time, Dolfie managed to secure a false identity card for Mira. It claimed that she was an eighteen-year-old Christian named Marienka Patzigová.

Shani was scared that Mira would not be able to pull off the ruse. He was likewise pretending to be Christian and had managed to quell rumours that he was really Jewish by going to church and delivering a perfect rendition of 'Ave Maria'. He wanted to demonstrate to his sister how she should act if she was ever at a church on her own. Together, during one of his visits home, the two of them paid a visit to one, and Mira learned how to cross herself with her right hand, and the proper way to receive the sacramental wine and bread offerings from the priest.

It was decided that Mira should live under her false identity in another town, where she could rent a room in a house and be secure. Sečovce was relatively far, but the family had an acquaintance there, Mr Winter, who had owned one of the biggest wholesale fabric stores in Slovakia, now aryanised. Mira, as Marienka, would go and work there. It gave Dolfie some solace to know that Martin Korn, a Jewish boy from their town, was also employed in the store using false documentation.

Mira began her first day in the new job wearing clothes from her sister Olga's wardrobe, trying to make herself look convincing as an eighteen-year-old, despite being two years younger. Her tasks were to write up the store's invoices and prepare paperwork for banking, and it turned out that she was an efficient worker. She was given her own office, and Mr Winter was pleased. Whenever his family hosted Yom Tov holiday meals, he asked her to join them, and she would briefly enjoy the chance to eat good food and let her guard down. Mostly, she was on high alert, careful about whom she socialised with. She deliberately befriended non-Jewish girls who were dark-haired and olive-skinned, because with her hazel eyes and brown hair she easily fit in among them. It would raise fewer questions about her real identity, she figured, than if she was being compared with a fairer, Germanic-looking group.

The only bothersome thing about her work was the persistent attention of another Jewish male co-worker whom Mira found to be pushy and rude. She tried complaining to her friend Martin, who then confided Mira's real age to this man, reasoning that he would leave her alone when he realised how young she was. But this strategy backfired; once he discovered she was Jewish, the man's intentions grew more serious.

Without Mira's knowledge, he travelled to Spišská Stará Ves alone. There he found Dolfie and professed his love for Mira, asking for her hand in marriage. 'We don't make arrangements for our children,' said Dolfie, fobbing him off. When the man returned to work, he presented Mira with a box containing cheesecake that Genya had baked. Mira was horrified that he had done this, telling him plainly that there was no future between them. An omen helped seal the message: when they opened the box together, they saw that the cheesecake was covered in ants that had made their way inside during his journey.

While she was living alone in Sečovce, Dolfie visited Mira once and tried to press some money on her. She refused, reminding him that she earned her own wages. What she didn't tell him was that sometimes they weren't enough to cover the necessities, and she was occasionally left hungry. But she was resourceful, and sewed herself a blouse and skirt by hand with pieces of fabric she was given from the store. She did not want to ask her parents for a cent. It gave her a unique sense of satisfaction to be so independent and make do on her own.

* * *

After three months of living away, new documents arranged by Dolfie allowed Mira to return to her family home in Spišská Stará Ves. She noticed how her parents had aged in her absence: both in their fifties, they looked worn and grey. Neighbours had always described Dolfie as 'cheerful' and 'witty', but that was in the distant past.

With no one around of her own age, Mira had few opportunities for socialising. One man, a thirty-two-year-old lawyer from a neighbouring town, began inviting her for walks. Although he was twice her age, it was wartime, and what would once have been unusual felt less so. He was interesting and intelligent, so she was pleased to stroll by his side and exchange ideas with him, but she only thought of him as a friend.

She did feel somewhat romantically towards a twenty-two-year-old fellow who would come to her family's store from another village to buy swatches of material. The first time he walked into the shop, her father sidled up next to him. Under his breath, Dolfie uttered one word by way of a question. *'Amcha?'* It was a Hebrew expression that meant: One of us? Are you Jewish? The young man nodded: yes.

Mira tried to make sure he did not catch her staring, but she couldn't help noticing his good looks.

The family invited him to join them for a meal, and he gave Mira his address. Soon, they were writing letters to each other. Mira did not know it then, but in less than two years' time, when the war was over, he would come to find her and immediately ask if he could kiss her. But by the end of the war, Mira was still only eighteen, and she had never been kissed before. She felt shy around him and was too embarrassed to give him permission. Even though she wanted him to kiss her, she said no.

* * *

In 1977, when I was eleven, I went to my first boy-girl party, a disco, where I only knew the twelve-year-old host. I was surprised when each of the six boys there asked me to dance, waiting their turn so that they could shuffle with me to the tunes of KC and the Sunshine Band and Donna Summer. The girls at the party all wore similar outfits: full, mid-calf skirts and flouncy shirts. I stood out in a striped, hooded t-shirt and white pants, and so the boys' attention was confusing; it was clear to me, at least, that I did not fit in. My parents had never said anything about my appearance. I arrived home from the party that evening and studied myself in the mirror: what had made the boys approach me? Did I look appealing? Or was it merely that I was the new girl? I had no idea how to assess it and I had no one to ask.

A few months later, one of those boys asked me to 'go around'. It meant that we had official boyfriend-girlfriend status, and would hold hands as we walked to the school bus at the day's end. It took me a while to tell my mother, and when I did, she seemed to disapprove, as I'd expected. For the next few years, whenever I was pursued by boys, she acted similarly, and so I learned to be evasive and secretive. I longed for a mother who would giggle with me about my crushes, hug me after my first kiss. But Mira was never like that.

Years later, I confronted her about it, still angry. Why hadn't she been more supportive of my early romances, perhaps guiding me through them so I might have better identified those boys who would not treat me well, forever sullying those early memories of first flirtations? But I had never seen it from her perspective, and she explained it to me: she had largely missed out on the experience of courtship in her teenage years and on those years entirely. Lacking a template for any of it, she distrusted it.

Twelve

Murky stories began floating around. Polish officers had fled a camp, and there were rumours that conditions were atrocious, but no one knew the details. Not long afterwards, Dolfie was speaking to his contact at the gendarmerie who had some news: two young Jewish men had been captured crossing the border from Poland to Slovakia illegally. They were taken to a holding pen in a state building rather than a prison, and apparently had wild tales about escaping from a concentration camp. 'Would you allow me to speak with them?' asked Dolfie. The contact agreed, and Mira accompanied him to where the pair was held.

It was around nine o'clock in the evening when they went; night had fallen. Mira sat quietly as her father asked questions, and the fellows told the same story over and over. In these camps, where they had been for some time, Jews were being killed. In Mira's recollection, they said, 'You don't get anything to eat. You work very hard. You get shot for no reason whatsoever. If the German looks at you and he doesn't like your face, he shoots you. If the German thinks you can't walk anymore, he shoots you. People die [for just] walking around.' It confirmed Dolfie's worst fear: dying did not seem to be a consequence of these camps; it was the whole point of them.

Heshek later recorded the name of the camp they said they had been in: Auschwitz. He and Dolfie at first tried to secure the men's release by bribing the jailer; a plan was hatched wherein the guard's hands would be tied, so he could pretend that the two escapees had overpowered him. But in the end, the Jewish functionaries of the town arrived at a different solution. A small amount of money was slipped to the men by Mr Mangel, which they put into their pockets. Someone had a contact in the border police, and a bribe resulted in a deal: the pair was charged with the crime of foreign-currency smuggling rather than for escaping Auschwitz. They had to stay in jail for a short term, on the condition that they return to Poland when the sentence was served. Needless to say, they never did so.

Mira never learned their names, but it seems likely that the men she had come face to face with were Arnošt Rosin, thirty-one, and Czesław Mordowicz, twenty-four. Two famous Jewish Auschwitz inmates with whom they were friendly – Rudolf Vrba and Alfred Wetzler – had escaped Auschwitz already, and Rosin and Mordowicz followed less than two months later, utilising a cramped hiding spot before fleeing themselves on 27 May 1944. Despite being so detailed in their account, they found that they were often met with disbelief. Many people were shocked, then distrustful. Not Dolfie Blumenstock. There was danger everywhere, Dolfie knew. He was no longer persuaded that everybody who had been taken away was safe. Around the same time, his son Heshek also told him about an acquaintance of his, a Polish man named David Milgrom, who claimed to have escaped from a purpose-built death camp. Heshek himself found it hard to believe his story. The Nazis were terrible, but this was unimaginable evil. Still, David's tale bothered him and stayed in a part of Heshek's brain that would not forget it, and so one day he recited it to his father, hoping that Dolfie would reassure him: surely no such killings were happening. That was not the response he received.

'I want to speak to him myself,' said Dolfie. 'I want to hear the story from his mouth.'

A meeting was arranged, and David relayed the horrors he had seen. Dolfie could see that David was an upstanding, honest young man; his parents had died before the war, leaving him in charge of his younger siblings. Dolfie had no reason to doubt him.

But Dolfie was dumbfounded by the reaction he received when he tried to warn others. Mira said, 'He told whoever would listen, but nobody wanted to believe it. People did not believe. I remember when he told Mr Strumpf, who said, "Ah, who knows? Maybe they just wanted to scare you. It can't exist that somebody is going around just shooting people. What are we now, living in the Old Ages time again? It's the twentieth century, don't you know?"'

This was a refrain uttered again and again. 'It's the twentieth century!' Or, 'The Germans are educated people! They are a top nation! They are humanitarians and so good at music and everything else – why would they want to do something like that?' Nobody wanted to hear otherwise.

Even Mira herself was not convinced where the truth lay. But Dolfie stood firm. 'My father said that one should listen to this. And take precautions. He said that to us all the time. He said, "If anything happens – if we are in danger … each of us should look only after themselves. You should not look [to see if] I am left behind, or your Mama is left behind. You should just save yourselves." He said that to each and every one of us. He said that many, many times.'

Thirteen

End of August 1944. Allied invasions of Western Europe had been taking place since June. Underground Slovak resistance units were rising up against the Slovak government, which was collaborating with Germany. None of this made the Blumenstocks feel any more secure. All around Slovakia, the atmosphere was heavy and dark. Everyone felt the unrest, and that meant that anything could happen.

Dolfie understood that Hitler and the Nazis were getting more desperate; it was impossible to predict what they might do. With the exception of Olga, he had managed to keep all in his immediate family from being deported, but time was running out. He tried to arrange escape via Turkey, but that had been thwarted when the Germans entered Hungary. He therefore needed to execute a more serious plan for hiding.

Soon, everything was in place. On his go-ahead, a horse and carriage with driver – arranged by non-Jewish neighbours – would take his family to a town two hours away. The Blumenstocks would travel very early in the morning, disguised as peasants so as to not raise suspicion. At their destination, everything had been set up so that the family could stay there for months, rather than days. Shani was set to meet them at the other end. They had prepared special clothes: garments that were older and looked dirty for the outer layers, but underneath they would wear items that had money and pieces of gold sewn into them. Genya had Napoleonic gold coins worth a small fortune, while American dollars were tucked inside a slit in the shoulder pads of Mira's jacket. There was also money in Mira's undergarments, and another wad of cash in a second bra that she could wear around her waist, beneath her skirt. Coins were even concealed in the heels of her shoes. Each member of the family had outfits that were loaded up this way, and they knew that in the event of an emergency, or if anything unexpected were to happen before their departure, they were to grab their clothes at once and immediately get dressed.

Everything was ready, but Dolfie was not. His son Heshek, set to join them, had been waylaid in Kežmarok. Each morning, Heshek would call on the store's telephone to say that he was stuck one day longer. Mira would listen to these calls and feel her face prickling with fresh terror every time. *Something is going to happen. Something is going to happen.* She tried to push away those thoughts, reminding herself of how often the family had dodged something bad, how their instincts had always been correct. But she nevertheless wore this terrible feeling like a tourniquet.

She felt so strongly that danger was imminent that after the third of Heshek's phone calls she asked her father: 'Papa, why do we have to wait for Heshek? We should just go to the new hiding spot *now*. We will tell him where we are going.

Or Mr Scholcz can tell him where we are. He can join us there. We shouldn't wait for him to make the journey with us.'

Dolfie looked at Genya and smiled. 'Your daughter is not stupid,' he said. 'I think she is right.'

And so they decided that this would be the last evening in their home. For the past four nights, Dolfie, Genya, Yanchi and Mira had been sleeping in their barn's loft, whose entrance Dolfie had extended so that all four could climb in. Feeling certain that they could be taken by German SS at any time, they no longer attended the store or stayed in the main house. They only came down to do necessary things, and did so quietly, creeping around as noiselessly as possible. Otherwise, they remained out of sight.

But on this night, 3 September, they had a different routine. Their Jewish neighbours knew they were leaving, and wanted to bid them farewell. The Blumenstocks agreed that everyone should join them for one last supper. Although the 8 p.m. curfew was in place, one could occasionally defy it because according to Mira, 'After eleven, there was not even a dog on the streets.' Among the guests were Dr Alexander Küchel and his wife. Dr Küchel was a well-respected man with a public profile, the only physician to have served the region for two decades. A prominent person in the Jewish *kehilla* – the Jewish congregation – he had also been a member of the district council and head of the fire department. His two sons and his brother lived with him. Bela Árje, who was not from Spišská Stará Ves but had done army service there as a young man; Mr Strumpf and his wife; and Mr and Mrs Mangel, who had once owned the inn next to the Blumenstocks, and their son, who had been unwell, now recovering. There was a young man, newly married; a wartime love story with a twist. He had agreed to wed Livia 'Lilly' Zipser, a friend of Olga's, so she could be under his protection, thus saving her from being taken away.

In the remaining group of Jews was a wealthy clan that owned much farm land, which included a saw mill, distillery and liquor store. In addition to the parents, there were nine children. One of their sons, forty-six-year-old Josef, was the town's adviser for agricultural matters, and a bachelor at the start of the war. He had also been urged to take a Jewish bride in order to save her life. Theirs was a happy marriage, and Josef had a baby girl born early that year, whom he adored.

Not everyone came to say goodbye to the Blumenstocks. Josef, for instance, was at the inn instead. But around half-a-dozen families turned up; together they played cards, ate something light, embraced. Everyone wished Mira and her family well. The end of the war must not be too far off. They would see each other again when it was over. For a brief moment, Mira allowed herself to think of what that might be like. Perhaps they would soon be reunited with her sister, Olga, and she and her friend Lilly could once again exchange confidences. Perhaps, perhaps.

When the last person left, it was close to midnight. This was far later in the evening than they were used to going up to the loft, which was still hard for Genya to manage. Dolfie was not much better at it and so made a decision: 'Let's sleep in the house tonight, in our bedroom. The horse and cart comes early to collect us. We will have to be ready at five in the morning. Let us sleep here for a few short hours.'

And so they undressed and made themselves comfortable. None of them could fall asleep easily; the goodwill of their evening was still with them, the adrenaline that came with the anticipation of the next morning's plans arriving afresh.

Then – suddenly – a loud noise broke the night's stillness. They all bolted upright. It was one o'clock in the morning. Someone was knocking on the gate to their garden and calling loudly, 'Partisans!' And then, louder still: '*Otworzyć!*' Open up!

It was a man speaking Polish, and so Dolfie was somewhat relaxed. 'Don't worry, Genya,' he told his wife. 'The partisans have always said that if they need anything, they will come to my house.' His relationship with the non-Jewish partisans was well-established by then. There was nothing to fear.

Mira held her breath as Yanchi moved to open the door. She started to put on her prepared clothes. It seemed like an emergency.

* * *

Earlier that evening, Josef was getting ready to leave the inn. It was late, and with a young baby at home he was unlikely to get unbroken sleep as it was. But abruptly, at the entrance: uniformed German SS officers, carrying rifles. They were on a mission, he could see that from the outset. The first thing they asked, addressing everyone in the inn: 'Is there a Jew here?' The new owners of the inn did not hesitate, nodding in Josef's direction immediately. 'Yes, he is Jewish.'

The officers, several of them, closed in on him, their weapons drawn. There had been a tip-off: a German man living in Spišská Stará Ves had gone to Nowy Targ in occupied Poland, informing the SS there that there were still eight Jewish families in his town. Now they demanded that Josef point out all the houses in the area where Jewish people lived. Josef knew he had no choice – apart from being at gunpoint, all the locals knew that this street was a Jewish one – but he tried to think quickly, to assess his options. Mira heard later that he'd made a bargain with those officers: 'I will tell you whatever you want, but I have one request to make. I have a baby daughter, and if I am to be taken with you, I hope that you will allow me to leave her with my neighbours.' Historically, the SS were not given to bargaining, but perhaps a bribe was offered as an incentive. At any rate, the houses were all only a short distance away. Two in particular were close to the inn. Across the road was the house belonging to Lilly Zipser and her husband. But Josef pointed first to the house right next door. The home of the Blumenstock family.

* * *

Many decades later, Mira would say something about this night. 'Everything in life is a coincidence.' What she meant: if Heshek had managed to come home earlier. If their friends hadn't stayed so late. If her family had not decided to sleep in their beds that night. If there had been no tip-off. If the officers had arrived in her town a day later. If Josef had not gone to the inn. If another house was chosen first. Coincidence? Bad luck? She never tried to assess it. Only to remember it as it happened.

* * *

'*Otworzyć! Otworzyć!*' The same words were shouted over and over from outside, but Dolfie felt no panic. 'It's all right, Yanchi,' he told his youngest son. 'You can open the door.' Yanchi was dressed for bed, wearing only a nightshirt and no pants. He approached the entrance, when at once there came the racket of their front gate being broken down. Dolfie now realised who had been calling out. Not partisans. Not Polish men. Armed German SS officers, fast approaching his house. He bolted down the hallway to the kitchen at its end; perhaps he could still save his family. Perhaps there was something he could do to help: run away, provide a distraction, or buy time so that at least Genya and Mira might flee in another direction. He had told his family over and over: *every man for himself.* He was likely imagining that the women were out the back door, running to safety. Maybe he was hoping to surprise the SS from their rear. Whatever the case, he launched himself through the kitchen window.

Genya and Mira, already dressed in the clothes they had thought to put on with the first knock at the gate, also remembered that rule. *Save yourself first.* But before Mira had time to do anything, she heard a bang. An unmistakable sound; it could not have been anything else. So loud that she still thought she could hear it long after it happened. She could feel its vibrations. She would feel it for days. She would feel it for years, for decades.

A gunshot.

It was so loud that it alerted Lilly and her husband across the road. Bela Árje, too, heard the noise. All of them managed to run away. Further down the street was Dr Küchel. When the SS arrived at his door, the doctor and his wife answered it.

But their son Otto, twenty at the time, and his uncle Mikulas both acted instinctively when they heard the rap on the door. Realising something was amiss because visitors would never appear at that hour, Otto escaped to a balcony at the back of the house, while Mikulas hid under a large table inside. Otto's parents were taken, together with his youngest brother, Tomas. Otto and his uncle were safe.

Dolfie had seen the Germans at his front door, but not the one who was lurking at the side. He was shot immediately. But he did not die immediately. He was still breathing, and began to moan. Genya knew that she was meant to run away and not look back. So did Mira. But neither of them could move, not with Dolfie still alive on the path in front of their house, and not with the moaning; his awful, unbearable moaning.

Genya ran to him, crying and calling out his name, 'Dolfie, Dolfie.' She went to cradle him, to kiss him. The German who was standing closest pushed her with his rifle butt. Mira tried to go to her father, but she too was shoved away and that was another moment she always remembered bitterly. 'He pushed me away with his gun, not even with his hand.'

Yanchi was briefly allowed to dress, under guard, and by the time they were marched away, Dolfie lay dead on the ground, a pool of blood around him. Mira wondered what would happen to him. She had a strange thought as she felt the chill of the night: she hoped her father would not be too cold.

Part Two

Fourteen

I never knew my grandfather Dolfie, but his death was always an integral part of my own origin story. How do Jewish people face death? In Jewish law, there is a list of rules that need to be followed pertaining to burial, mourning and even the way the body is handled at the time of death. When somebody takes their final breaths – if you know their death is imminent, and it is the last minutes of their life – you are not allowed to leave the room unless there are exceptional circumstances. It is considered a mark of deep respect to watch over someone as they pass over from this world to the next one.

When death has been established, the eyes and mouth of the person must be closed, the body orientated so that their feet face the doorway. The body's placement can only be changed if it is a matter of honour – if they have died in an awkward position, for example. A candle is placed near their head; some mourners place candles all around the body. This is the time for loved ones to ask the deceased for forgiveness.

From the moment the person dies until they are buried, they are not allowed to be left alone. Someone is chosen to remain next to them at all times – a *shomer*, or watcher. The function began as a practical one in olden times – the corpse had to be guarded so that it was not set upon by thieves or rats – but has become tradition: the *shomer* performs a spiritual role, acting as a guardian of the dead, whose soul might be hovering until burial.

Integral to Jewish belief is the idea of an afterlife. If leaving their mother's womb is the birth of the physical body, then leaving the physical body is the untethering of a person's soul. Life is but a short, finite preparation for the vast world beyond.

* * *

There they were – Mira, Genya and Yanchi – with the handful of other Jews who had also been discovered and caught. First they were taken to a building belonging to the gendarmerie. Genya was very, very quiet. They sat in a room together, the door shut. They were not sure who was guarding it. They were not sure how many guards there were.

Yanchi kept looking around, trying to peer out of a window, his expression unreadable. He moved closer to his mother and whispered to her, 'Mama, should I try to run away?'

Genya sighed. 'Yanchi,' she said, 'have a look at what happened to your father. How can I say you should run away? I don't know what will be, but maybe the chances are better if you stay here.'

He didn't raise the subject again.

It proved to be a brief stop. From there, the entire group was taken directly to Nowy Targ in occupied Poland, where they were put into prison. Men and women were separated, and since Jews from neighbouring towns had also been rounded up, Mira found herself crammed in a cell with almost a dozen females and only two beds. It was pandemonium, with all the women vying for a mattress; it was that or sleep on the floor. 'It's strange how even in the worst situations, people fight for comfort,' she said. Seventeen-year-old Mira, the youngest there, was aghast. Her father had just been murdered, and these women were fighting over a *bed*?

'I don't know where I took the courage from, but I got up and I said, in a very firm, strong voice: "*I* will tell you who will sleep in those beds."'

Everyone looked at her and stopped arguing immediately. She was small in stature, but there was something formidable about her.

Mira gestured to a woman she knew from her town; she was eighty years old and crippled. 'Mrs Špira is going to sleep in this bed.' She then singled out another elderly woman to occupy the second one. 'Everyone else will sleep on the floor.'

Nobody argued. There was such command in her voice, and since the rest could see the wisdom in her decision, they deferred to it immediately.

Mira settled down on the floor herself, leaning against her mother. Soon, her eyes closed and she fell into a deep sleep, her head tipping into Genya's lap. She did not wake up for many hours. When she finally did so, she could see that while she had managed to lie down, her mother was still upright and had clearly been so the whole night. Genya had not dared to move, lest she wake her daughter.

Once Mira realised this, she started to cry bitter tears. 'I felt so guilty. I had made sure other people were comfortable but not my own mother?' She sobbed to Genya, 'Mama! I did not look after you. Why didn't you wake me?' Genya shushed her, and put her arms around her. 'It is all right, Mirush,' she said. 'Don't worry, don't worry. You are a good girl, you did nothing wrong.' But Mira could not be comforted, not even when she had long surpassed Genya's age of fifty-two. As an old lady herself, Mira said, 'I still can't forgive myself. It was so terrible. That she did not want to move because of me? That's what hurt me. My poor mother.'

* * *

Later on, Mira would develop a great talent for comforting; perhaps she had it all along. I like to think that Genya watched her sleeping daughter – peaceful under the least peaceful of circumstances – and found some consolation in that. When it came to mothering her own children, there was no one better at changing their moods from bad to good; no one whose murmurs of sympathy and understanding could so easily act as a balm. Mira had a secret way of soothing her grandchildren, too: more than one of them sought her out when they needed help through a dark patch. She would coax them gently out of the shadows, partly through her sensible, wise words, but also by offering her brand of warm and unquestioning compassion.

Fifteen

The group of Jewish prisoners was soon herded to their next destination. It would be a concentration camp: Plaszow, which housed somewhere between two and five thousand prisoners at the time the Blumenstocks arrived; around twenty thousand had been deported to other camps the month before.

Plaszow became known to mainstream audiences as one of the settings in Steven Spielberg's movie *Schindler's List*, based on Thomas Keneally's non-fiction book, *Schindler's Ark*. The Nazis operated more than forty thousand camps in World War II: Plaszow was situated in Kraków, in occupied Poland's south. Originally a forced labour camp, Plaszow had become an effective killing operation. In 1944, building materials had been hauled in so that a crematorium could be built. Although it was included in the blueprints for the camp, it never went ahead. There were other ways to get rid of bodies, it turned out.

The commandant of the camp, Austrian SS-Hauptsturmführer Amon Göth, was notorious even beyond the boundaries of Plaszow for his inhumane acts, his blood-thirstiness, his viciousness. Göth routinely tortured Jews, set dogs upon them and murdered them. Not long before Mira's arrival there, Göth had devised the 'kindergarten' trap. He told parents that their children would be sent to a newly established camp kindergarten (*Kinderheim*) while their elders slaved away at hard labour by day. It was presented as a benefit: there, the children would experience far more humane conditions. These families were shown the grounds, and saw an airy new block which would be the 'clubhouse', a playground in front of it. But on 14 May, the SS rounded up three hundred small children from the *Kinderheim* and put them onto trucks. Their parents could see their little ones from where they stood at the compulsory *Appellplatz*, the punishing daily roll call, but were not allowed to go to their youngsters, who had started to shake and sob. Those who dared try were beaten with truncheons. Suddenly a children's song began to play over the camp's loudspeakers – 'Mutti Kauf mir ein Pferdchen' or, 'Mummy, Buy me a Pony'. With this jaunty tune for a soundtrack, the parents watched in horror as the children were driven away. They knew what that meant. There would be nothing left to live for after their children had met such a terrible end.

* * *

The timing was fortuitous: after a nineteen-month tenure, Göth would leave his post of commandant just a few days after the three Blumenstocks arrived. Perhaps the prisoners at

Plaszow thought that, even though Göth's ruthless accomplices remained, conditions would be marginally better.

Genya, Yanchi and Mira were immediately separated as the newcomers were divided into groups of men and women, each ordered to stand in straight rows. Mira huddled close to her mother in a group of about forty females. An SS officer shouted instructions: 'Twenty men and twenty women will stay, and the rest of you will go to another camp because there is no room here.' Mira and Genya were at the front of the line, but when the guard started counting, he did so from the back. *One, two, three …* until he got to twenty. Mira and her mother had missed out on that first group, and so found themselves boarding the truck bound for the work camp.

Genya was the first to climb into the vehicle, and Mira stood behind, her hand on her mother's back to help her up the steps. Then it was Mira's turn. She had one foot on the truck when she was suddenly grabbed from behind.

It was the SS guard, swiftly yanking her back to the ground. *'Du bleibst hier!'* he commanded. You stay here!

Mira dared to protest. 'I want to go with my mother!' she cried.

Instead of replying, the SS man shouted an order to the driver. *'Abfahren!' Drive away!* He turned to Mira and repeated, 'You stay here. You are number twenty-one.'

Before the truck drove off, Mira managed to untie the money-stuffed bra from around her waist, thrusting it at Genya. 'Take this,' she said. 'I've got enough. You will need it more than me.' She hoped that it might enable her mother to buy some unimagined advantage.

* * *

Here is what Mira looked like when she arrived at Plaszow. She was a slight seventeen-year-old who appeared much younger, easily passing for fifteen. She had thick wavy hair that fell past her shoulders. Her eyes were light brown. She had deep dimples and a heart-shaped face, and she was beautiful. Did that make a difference? Was it possible that the guard felt sympathy for her when so few in his position would have done? Admired her? Did Mira's appearance serve to distinguish her – she who had been fed and nourished and nurtured until this point of the war – from the longer-serving female prisoners at Plaszow, who were so sickly and ravaged that they already looked half-dead?

Later, Mira would say that the SS officer had saved her life. She did not know why – 'maybe he saw a young girl and took pity'. She never found out who he was, or saw him again. She believed that he potentially put himself at risk by making her an extra inmate: number twenty-one when only twenty females were to be left behind.

At the time, Mira did not know where her mother was headed, but she found out later from her Polish cousin Moshe Sperling, who had been in the camp for far longer than she. In a different part of Plaszow lay an open pit, with a plank across the hole. It was one of several execution sites that existed in the camp by that time. Each of the men and women on that truck – including Genya – was ordered to strip naked before walking along the plank. Before they reached the end, shots were fired. If they were lucky, they died instantly, falling into the mass grave below, a heap of rotting bodies. But some were not so fortunate. Those prisoners who later had the gruesome task of covering over the corpses with handfuls of soil to bury them reported that in some areas of the pit there was still movement. 'The earth was moving for days,' they said.

* * *

How does anyone survive living through this time, losing both their parents this way? I could never understand it. I know that my mother was unable to tell a story about my grandparents without returning to their sad endings, although she did not cry when she spoke about them. Rather, she concentrated on their light: the cheerful, tinkling laugh of her father, the warm heart of her mother. It is much more important to remember how people have lived, she taught me, than to remember how they died. I know that when she went to *shule* four times each year to say *Yizkor* – the Jewish memorial prayers – she would clench her hand into a fist and bang it against her heart in the rhythm of the Hebrew words of mourning, as was usually the custom for reciting the Yom Kippur Day of Atonement prayers. That was the only time she allowed the tears to come.

Sixteen

Before she was sent to her barrack, Mira was ordered to strip naked and wash. But harsh warnings came from all the officials along the way: If you possess any money or valuables, you must give them up immediately. Failure to do so will be punished by death. When Mira undressed and put her clothes in a pile, she was seized by the fear that the dollars and coins concealed in her garments would be found, especially given that she had to leave her clothes behind while she entered the showers. She quickly sought out the *Lagerälteste*, the camp elder who was in charge of ensuring the prisoners' zone ran smoothly. It was the highest rank a prisoner could hold and it came with certain privileges, such as access to a private room. This female *Lagerälteste* was Jewish, and Mira told her that she had money stashed away. 'Give it to me,' she said, 'and I will hand it over. Do not worry. You will be fine.' Mira did as she was told, then showered and went to her barrack.

By the time she got there, word had spread to the other prisoners about what had happened. Mira had forfeited around US$500 – a small fortune today. 'Are you crazy?' one of them asked. 'The *Lagerälteste* is never going to give it to the Germans. She will put it in her own pocket. You could have had it much easier here if you'd kept it for yourself.'

The next day, the camp's top *Kapo*, a handsome German man named Erich,* marched into the barrack. His manner was menacing. 'Which of you handed over money yesterday?' he boomed. 'If you tell me, I will help you.'

There was silence, even though all the women knew who had done so. Mira herself was too scared to speak up.

Erich continued, sterner. 'If you do not give yourself up, you will be punished severely.' Prisoners had been tortured or shot for lesser transgressions, such as smuggling in extra bread.

With that, Mira stepped forward. 'It was me.'

'Ach, so you are the *Dollarprinzessin*, the Dollar Princess,' said Erich, looking her over. 'Because you came forward, I will look after you.'

Now Mira was even more terrified. She wasn't sure what he meant by this, but she knew it was nothing good.

* * *

On the other side of the camp, in the men's barracks, Yanchi – who had also been counted among the twenty male prisoners allowed to stay at Plaszow - was similarly scared that the valuables sewn into his own clothes would be uncovered. Since he did not know what to do, he confided in Josef,

---

* This was likely to have been Erich Harder (born in 1905) who was the camp's head *Kapo* from August 1944.

the man who had pointed out his parents' house to the SS. The Blumenstocks never condemned him for this; as Mira said, 'If he had not shown them, somebody else would have done so. Nobody thought he could do anything about it. He was not responsible.' Josef had a solution. 'Don't worry – give it to me. I will hide it for you and we will share it.' He kept his word, and later the two men would hand those dollars to male prisoners who worked outside of the camp – toiling in stone quarries, for example – in exchange for bread or cigarettes.

Whenever this occurred, Yanchi made sure to share the spoils with Mira in the evening, when the siblings were able to walk along the pathway leading to the other's barrack and meet in the middle for the briefest of exchanges. While the food in camp had slightly improved since Göth had left – now including items such as powdered milk and sugar – it was still strictly rationed, and most prisoners received meagre portions. Mira never forgot the day when her brother came and handed her some soft bread with scrambled egg, a luxury she could barely remember existed. This was as miraculous as if a heater suddenly appeared in her bed to warm her toes. 'Yanchi, how did you get this?' she asked.

And he explained: he had been made to work in a punishing, labour-intensive task that required his full effort. He was one of the stronger men at camp; certainly among the fittest, with his previous soccer training. As he worked, the German supervisors kept pushing him to exert himself further, to go more quickly, screaming, '*Schneller, schneller!*' After a time, he stopped, exhausted. 'How can I work quicker?' he asked. 'I am trying, but I cannot do any more than I already am.' Whether he was firm or polite, Mira never said, but there was a startling response: the two men in charge spoke to him as if he were human, not beast. They knew he was doing his best, they assured him, and then they invited him to share their lunch, offering him two slices of bread with the cooked egg. He gobbled down some, putting the other half into his pocket. It was this portion that he gave to Mira.

* * *

Erich was not the only one who knew that Mira had arrived at Plaszow with money. Once, when she was working, two Wehrmacht supervisors – soldiers who served in the German army – passed by. Calling her over, one asked, 'Did you come with somebody to camp, a mother?'

'Yes.'

The two men exchanged looks, and the one who had spoken to Mira muttered in German, '*Ich habe dir gesagt, dass muss sie sein.*' *I told you this must be her.* He then turned to Mira and said something that made her feel cold with shock: 'She said we should look after you.' And then the soldiers moved on.

Mulling over this exchange later, Mira believed she knew what happened. Right before Genya's death, her mother must have realised her fate. Knowing that she had Mira's bra with all its money inside, Mira thought that Genya quickly handed it to a supervisor, pleading with them to look after her daughter back in camp. Mira could never be sure, but it made sense: why else would they make a connection to her? 'At least I knew that,' she said, by which she meant: at least I knew my mother was thinking about me, caring for me, right up until the end.

* * *

Despite the fact that she had to share a mattress with another girl, occasionally Mira slept deeply and dreamed about her mother. Genya would appear and hold her daughter in her arms. Once or twice, Mira would be sitting in a warm bath, while Genya ran a soapy washcloth down the length of her body in gentle strokes. Mira could not always remember what was said in those dreams, or their exact details, but she woke up feeling her mother's caress, and the restorative warmth of her mother's love.

* * *

Some days, Mira performed small tasks at camp – cleaning, or carrying things from one place to another – but one time she was given the worst possible job. At the end of 1944, the Nazis were trying to conceal all traces of their crimes, and so they forced male prisoners to dig up the older mass graves. The men would have to pick up the corpses and carry them away to be burned on a pyre. As Mira recalled, 'We were the group of girls who had to put the soil back and refill the graves. The stench was terrible – it was soaked with the odour of dead bodies. And we often found a hand, or some hair, or teeth, or an eye – because when the boys took the corpses, some things fell away.'

She was filling a grave with sand when the *Kapo* Erich arrived with a member of the SS, accompanied by a young dog. Erich called out with a laugh, '*Nu, Dollarprinzessin* – at home you did not do a job like this, I'm sure.' And then he added, 'Forget about your work – go play with the dog.'

Mira obeyed, glad to leave the pit but not really wanting to play with the dog, either. It was rough and boisterous, the way some young dogs are, and that scared her. The dog didn't seem to like her particularly, perhaps because of the scent she carried on her. But the incident spared her thirty minutes of work, and for that she was grateful.

Even without Erich coming to her rescue, she was often given a slight reprieve when she was working on the graves. The Jewish *Kapo* in charge of that task, a man named Krakau, seemed to take pity on her, and he allowed her to leave five minutes before the other women. This might not sound like much, but for Mira it was a tremendous boon: it meant that she could go to the shower block before everyone else, and still have hot water with which to wash away the putrid smells on her. 'Those were little things, but they were extremely important to survive, and to feel that you are still a person.' By the time the other women arrived, they had to push and shove each other to get enough water. Mira had no idea why Krakau favoured her like this. 'In my life, in camp, I always had people who did things for me for no reason. They just felt sorry for me, or they felt an inclination to do something for me.'

When the heads of the camp decided to build a new *Appellplatz* – where prisoners stood for the daily roll call but were also routinely executed, or at the very least tormented, forced to stand for interminable periods under unbearable conditions – stones had to be moved from one location to the next. Mira was one of the women selected to both loosen and carry the stones – heavy work which often saw the malnourished prisoners keel over and collapse, thus marking them for execution. As she laboured, Erich walked past once more. He approached the supervising female *Kapo* and had a quiet word in her ear. She in turn beckoned Mira over and said, 'You can go back to the barracks. You can stay there, and you do not have to work. If someone asks what you are doing, say you have to clean up the rubbish that is scattered on the ground outside.' Mira looked at her puzzled, so the woman leaned in and said conspiratorially, 'You know you don't really have to do that, right? You can just rest.' Mira remembered how this had to be explained to her; the *Kapo* knew that she was bound to take everything at face value. 'I was so naive and ignorant that even she had to tell me: you don't have to pick it up.'

In addition, Erich handed her extra tickets, which were used in exchange for food rations. He gave her a slip of paper which meant that every Tuesday, when fresh bread was baked, she was allowed to collect a small loaf for herself and some of the women she shared quarters with. 'Do you know what that meant?' she marvelled. 'Nice, beautiful, hot, extra bread? Why he picked me, I don't know.'

* * *

Mira was so afraid that Erich's idea of looking after her would entail something debased or sinister that she never welcomed the sight of him. One day, when she was collecting stones right outside a room where the SS were stationed, she was 'petrified' when he summoned her inside. He brought her into his office and told her to sit on a chair facing him across the desk. She must have looked frightened, because he quickly reassured her. 'Don't worry,' he said. 'I am not going to do anything to you.' He held out a box of chocolates and urged her to take one. He asked how she was faring, and then he handed her a coupon, which he said could be exchanged for a new item of clothing at the storeroom. It was always a mystery to Mira why he acted this way. She later heard different rumours about why he was a prisoner – someone said he was a Communist; another thought he was homosexual. Whatever the case, he clearly did not desire her. Perhaps he thought she came from a wealthy family, given how willingly she'd handed over her hidden money. Or maybe he wanted to reward her for her honesty? She did not know.

She had no use for the coupon herself, but Yanchi had recently torn his jacket, so she gave it to him. He went to the storeroom, where clothes were displayed on hangers or folded into baskets. One did not ask where these clothes came from, for it was self-evident. They were the discarded garments of those who had been murdered, taken from them before their deaths.

Seventeen

Two weeks after Mira arrived at Plaszow, it was Rosh Hashanah, the Jewish New Year, which is traditionally honoured with a festive meal. Some of the women gathered in the barracks in the morning to say Hebrew prayers. Expressing one's Jewish identity in this way was punishable – sometimes by death – but many did it regardless. Mira did not see any *siddurs*, or prayer books, that had been illegally concealed, but plenty of the women there were so well versed in the prayers that they knew them by heart. Everyone was urged to save some food from their breakfast or lunch, so that they could eat more in the evening; by doing so, they could symbolically replicate the feast they might be enjoying at home. There would be no round challah bread baked with raisins to express their wish for a sweet new year, but still they could celebrate in this limited way.

Ten days later, another important event on the calendar: Yom Kippur, the Jewish Day of Atonement. On this day, Jews fast from dusk until dark, for twenty-five hours. During that time, neither food nor water is to pass one's lips. Mira took her potato out of that morning's soup and kept it in her pocket until night-time, fasting for the entire day, as did many of the other women. Although she was famished, she was determined to observe one of the holiest holidays in Judaism. She did so despite the fact that Jewish law allows for exemptions; health must always take priority over abiding to the rules. But Mira had another reason for fasting. She said, 'We thought that maybe it would help. That if we did whatever the religion asked of us, we might be saved. I believed very strongly in God, and there were quite a few others who felt the same. We did not take any notice of those who didn't, but I think that even those people felt good to hear the prayers.'

* * *

Not all Jewish people kept their faith during the Holocaust; many rejected any belief in God. But there was evidence that others still held strongly to the tenets of their religion through the very worst of moments. There are reports that Jews, on their way to the crematoria of the death camps, sang 'Ani Ma'amin', a hymn that carries the notion of the afterlife. *'Ani ma'amin be'emuna shelemah.'* I believe with complete faith in the coming of the Messiah, I believe.

And while prayer did not save those souls from being killed on earth, it did change the outcome for some of the youngest survivors. A story is told about Jewish children whose parents had hidden them with nuns and priests during the Holocaust. When the war ended, many of these families had been wiped out, so it was up to Jewish authorities to identify those who had been left behind. Since these children had been raised as Catholics in orphanages, the church was reluctant to hand them back so many years later: there was no documentation proving that they were born Jewish. But one rabbi in charge of seeking out such youngsters arrived at a monastery in Alsace-Lorraine with an idea: he started singing the *Shema*, the holy prayer. He reasoned that Jewish youngsters would likely remember the chant they had recited twice a day, including before bed every night. Suddenly, the children joined in, automatically crying out for their lost mothers when they heard the tune. Identity embeds itself in different ways: in sound, in feeling, in memory.

* * *

Outside the gates of Plaszow, the Soviet army was getting closer. The Germans took steps to dismantle the camp and eradicate any evidence of their crimes. The last prisoners would leave by January 1945, and all that would be left of Plaszow by the time the Red Army arrived later that month was a barren field. Mira and Yanchi, who had been there a little less than two months, were transferred to other camps beforehand.

Yanchi left first in the middle of October. He was not told his destination. Mira happened to be near the departure area when he was leaving, and saw him in the line of men waiting to board the truck. She was not allowed to approach him, but she could nevertheless call out some parting words. 'Yanchi, I hope to see you after the war,' she shouted. She knew how strong and capable he was; if anyone could survive, he could.

He was able to shoot back only three words to her in response. 'Look after yourself.'

She later found out that Yanchi was taken to Gross-Rosen, together with Josef. At this concentration camp, conditions were also inhumane, and the Nazi guards were known to be especially sadistic. Prisoners were pushed to their limits, some working on Hitler's network of underground tunnels and fortifications. They were banned from speaking to one another, and there was hardly any food.

After the war, Josef told Mira what had happened: within a very short time, Yanchi became a *Muselmann*, the term prisoners used to describe those who were so starved that they became skeletal, or when they grew so listless they became resigned to their fate. Yanchi had weakened quickly, growing more emaciated by the day; many prisoners in that camp died of starvation. However, someone else heard that he had injured his leg, and was shot because he could no longer work. Yanchi, the playmate of her youth – this handsome, charismatic, kind young man, the boy who could win anyone over and do every trick with a soccer ball – would die brutally at the age of twenty-one.

Eighteen

Less than a week after Yanchi's departure, in October 1944, Mira was taken to her next destination: Auschwitz II–Birkenau in occupied Poland. She would have passed through its entrance without being able to see it from her windowless cattle car, a reddish brick building surrounded by an electric barbed-wire fence. Auschwitz operated as both concentration and extermination camp, putting into place the plan known as *Endlösung der Judenfrage*, or the Final Solution to the Jewish Question – Hitler's goal for the genocide of all Jewish people. Around 1.1 million people would be murdered there. One million of those were Jews.

Auschwitz was the broader name given to three camps and a series of sub-camps in a complex that covered five hundred acres, but the Auschwitz-Birkenau killing centre was the deadliest. There the crematoriums, with furnaces for burning bodies, could burn 4416 corpses per day, according to the German authorities, but the Jewish prisoners who worked there called this an underestimation. Mira could still picture its tall chimneys decades later. Again, it was a matter of good timing: less than two weeks after she arrived at Auschwitz, the gas chambers were no longer used. With the Soviet forces getting closer, it was time for the Nazis to destroy the evidence of mass killing.

Mira had one friend by her side: Blanka Goldmann. The two had met up in Plaszow, and were grateful to have found each other. In the war, with so many relatives separated or killed, friends became family. The day they arrived at Birkenau, it was chilly. One hundred or so women had been deported along with Mira, and they were all made to stand at the *Appellplatz*, waiting for the roll call to start. They were there for over an hour and a half, shivering in the biting wind. It felt to Mira as though she would be standing there forever, each minute ticking slowly by. She could not imagine what lay ahead.

Suddenly, somebody was calling out: 'Is anybody here from Kežmarok, or a city in that vicinity?' It was a *Stubenälteste* who asked this, a prisoner assigned as the room leader at the camp. Mira raised her hand; Spišská Stará Ves was a neighbouring town, so she knew Kežmarok well. The *Stubenälteste* then led Mira away, saying, 'The *Blockälteste* wants to talk to you.' This title was given to the block elder, the prisoner who oversaw a single camp barrack.

Led into the wooden accommodation, she was shocked to see a familiar face. Edit Rose, petite with light grey-green eyes, her hair shorn, was three years older than Mira, and had lived just outside of Spišská Stará Ves, in Matiašovce. They were friendly acquaintances, and had many friends in common. Edit greeted Mira with relief, warmth and joy. 'Mira, you are here! My God! Don't worry – I will do whatever I can to help you.'

Mira was startled to find the other woman still alive. Edit had been on the very first transport to Auschwitz from Poprad, on 25 March 1942; it was now more than two and a half years later. Her tattooed number told the story of her early arrival: 1371. She had already been through so much, including being experimented upon by Carl Clauberg, a German gynaecologist who was prone to sterilising female prisoners in camp. Mira, freshly plucked from freedom and all its benefits – family, food, shelter – expected that Edit would be resentful after having served so much more time as a prisoner, but all Mira saw in her face was sincerity.

In her first act of kindness, Edit said: 'You can stay here with me, where it is warmer. When it is time for the roll call, you will go back. But you don't have to stand in the freezing cold for so long.' And that is what transpired. Edit supervised a transition block, specifically for new arrivals, with bunks spanning three levels, side by side. Mira stayed there for two weeks, and each night Edit allowed her into the private room that was one of the privileges of her rank. It was far better than her own cramped surroundings. Together, she and Edit would sing songs and exchange information about what had happened to the townspeople they knew. Often, the news was horrific. But generally they reminisced about happier times, and those nightly get-togethers were a welcome reprieve from the long days. They shared extra food, another advantage of Edit's status: whatever rations were left over after being distributed to the group became hers. It was not that much – perhaps two extra servings, those already tiny, of soup and scraps of bread –

but by the standards of Birkenau, this was a feast, and Edit's presence in the camp was an incredible stroke of good luck.

* * *

An entry from *The Auschwitz Chronicle*, 22 October 1944, an academic work produced by a Polish historian:

> *SS Camp Doctor Mengele conducts a two-hour selection among the female Jews sent from the Plaszow concentration camp. He sends 1765 women to Transit Camp 11c. The remaining women are killed in the gas chambers. Giza Landau, who arrives with this transport, receives No. A-26098 and another female Jew is given the No. A-27752.*[*]

Unbeknownst to Mira, she had been part of a 'selection', played almost like a macabre game of Russian roulette. Point at this person, they live. Point at another, they die. Not too long before the end of 1944, anyone who was deported to Auschwitz under the age of sixteen was automatically killed. Mira was seventeen. Perhaps she never knew how precariously close she came to being on the wrong side of the selection, where an average of 80 per cent of arrivals were sent to their deaths. On the day she arrived – who knows why? – only 20 per cent of women coming from Plaszow met this fate.

Nor did she ever mention that she had encountered the infamous Nazi doctor Josef Mengele, who was conducting

---

[*]   Danuta Czech (ed.), *Auschwitz Chronicle 1939–1945*. (Henry Holt and Company, New York, 1989, pp 737–738.)

the selection that day. He would remain there for several months after her arrival, performing his abominable medical experiments on prisoners, especially on twins – his fascination. He would often operate on young children, maiming or killing his subjects, sometimes hastening the latter to enable his post-mortem examinations.

But it seems that Mira had not recognised him. All her life, she had only heard about the *Malakh Ha-mavet*, the Angel of Death, who appeared in the Seder's last song every Passover. Here was someone who bore that moniker in real life. Was it lucky or unlucky that she was coming face to face with him on that day? Either way, this time she was spared.

* * *

What is good luck? How is it created? The concept of good luck seems woven into the fabric of Jewish people; the congratulatory expression '*mazel tov*' actually translates to 'good luck'. But the Torah specifies that luck is not something to be chased. A Jewish person's path should be determined by prayer and action rather than an esoteric idea of 'luck'.

Still, the number 18 is considered especially significant – the more secular Jews would say 'lucky' – representing *chai*, or life, and so when you make a donation to charity, it is customary to do so in multiples of 18, whether it's $36 or $180. When my daughter was born on the eighteenth of the month, Mira called her my triple-*chai* baby: not only due to her birth date, but because both of her English and Hebrew names – Zoë and Chaya – translated to 'life'. When I was pregnant, I learned the extent to which Jews are unwilling to rely on luck. No one says '*mazel tov*' to an expectant mother. Instead, one says '*b'sha'ah tovah*' – in good time.

Mira did not believe that good luck was something to be counted on. It could happen, yes, but in life you made your own luck. A constant refrain in my childhood were her words, drummed into her by Dolfie: 'Help yourself and God will help you.' She would assist her children only to a point. If you were able to achieve something on your own, you had better do so.

Nineteen

On 7 October 1944, a fortnight before Mira arrived at Auschwitz-Birkenau, a major rebellion had taken place – an uprising by the *Sonderkommando,* those Jewish prisoners whose role it was to remove corpses from the gas chambers before burning them. Realising they too would be killed eventually, they planned a mutiny. Explosives had been smuggled in by female prisoners working in forced labour at the Weichsel-Union-Metallwerke armaments factory, housed in Auschwitz. Their plan was ultimately to escape.

They were compelled to put their scheme into effect early, first attacking the SS with hammers and hatchets before setting Crematorium IV on fire. But they were no match for the machine guns and grenades they faced, and although three guards were killed, so were 451 of the prisoners, who either died during the fighting or were shot afterwards. Four Jewish women who brought in the explosives were publicly hanged.

One of these was twenty-four-year-old Roza Robota, who had been instrumental in the resistance. Roza worked in the clothing detail at Birkenau, and when the other women smuggled out gunpowder, they handed it to her. She then passed it along to her collaborators in the *Sonderkommando*. The SS had tortured Roza in an attempt to find out who else was part of her ring, but she refused to divulge any names. She was executed on the night of 6 January 1945. Mira saw her hanged, but she seldom spoke about it in the years afterwards. It was only decades later that she described the scene.

'After she was caught, they put her in a small cell. When they decided she was going to be hanged, we all had to be there to watch her. Her name will always be in my heart. She came out to the podium where the noose for the hanging was, and she walked straight and proud. When they started to put the noose around her neck, she lifted her head and she said in Polish – and I understand Polish – "*Zemsta!*" Revenge! She wanted us to avenge what was happening, she wanted us not to forget. We all have to do what we can to not let anything like that ever happen again. We are proud people, and should stay proud always.'

Witnessing this left Mira profoundly moved. 'We were all so very, very depressed, and so sad. The whole camp was crying for days. It affected us terribly. We saw that this beautiful young girl gave her life and was still strong enough to tell us to avenge her. She was incredible.'

* * *

Naturally, many prisoners could not cope with their ordeal. On one of Mira's first nights in Birkenau, a young Czech girl – perhaps fifteen, younger than Mira – lay in her bunk weeping pitifully. As the minutes ticked away and her cries would not subside, the other women shouted at her unsympathetically. 'We are going to tell on you! We are going to say that you are not letting us sleep!' But the girl only sobbed harder.

Approaching her bed, Mira – who knew the girl had also come from Plaszow – touched her shoulder. She started speaking to her in a soothing voice. 'Don't cry,' Mira said gently, as if talking to a small child. 'It doesn't help. We will be home one day, you will see.'

The girl's noises turned to soft whimpers, and Mira lay down next to her. Eventually, they both fell asleep.

A few days later, Mira realised she had gotten lice from her bed mate, and her head had to be shorn. She had been proud of her long hair beforehand, but that was on the outside, in freedom, in another world. She did not care about her hair anymore.

* * *

Even though Edit was fond of Mira's company, she was set on having her friend moved from Birkenau to Auschwitz I. Edit's barrack was designed for incoming prisoners, and Mira could not stay there long term. In one particular Auschwitz block, there was a *Blockälteste* and several *Stubenältestinnen* whom Edit knew from Kežmarok and its surrounds, and they would keep Mira safe.

It happened quickly enough: when fifteen women needed to be transferred, Edit included Mira and Blanka among them, although they did not go to Auschwitz I immediately. When they were asked what special qualifications they had,

Mira opted for agriculture, saying she could milk cows and work in the fields. She remembered something her father, Dolfie, had said when he still believed his children might be taken to labour camps: if they ever found themselves there, it was better to work on the open land, where a stray carrot or potato might be found. Blanka claimed that she was adept in agriculture as well, even though, according to Mira, 'She had never seen a cow before.' But they were determined to stick together. They were sent to one of Auschwitz's sub-camps and stayed on the land for three weeks. It was crippling work, requiring them to move large stones from one place to another. 'I don't know for what reason,' Mira said. 'There probably was no reason. But it was bad, because it was under even tighter scrutiny, and there were very vicious people there, so that we could not relax for a minute. People were falling like flies.' If the prisoners stopped working, they would be beaten. Mira was relieved when that job was over.

By this time, she and Blanka both looked like Auschwitz prisoners, dressed in the blue-and-white-striped prisoner's uniform: for women it was a dress, with two yellow triangles forming a Star of David sewn over the chest to indicate that they were imprisoned for being Jewish. While both girls made it to Auschwitz I, only Mira was transferred to the promised Block 1, in the *Schutzhaftlagererweiterung*, a new part of the expanded Auschwitz I camp, where a women's section had recently been constructed. Blanka was not as fortunate; she was sent to a different part of the camp, and was allotted night work in a factory. It was a cruel twist that the sign at Auschwitz's entrance – ARBEIT MACHT FREI – translated to 'Work will set you free'. Much of the work was so gruelling that it would only set people free from the earthly shackles of living. Blanka would have to labour all through the night and still stand on the *Appellplatz* for roll call when she returned, for hours at a time. Only then was she permitted to sleep, but never soundly; the noise of the camp disturbed her rest.

Mira, by contrast, had landed comparatively well. In Block 1, she said the female prisoners were not pushed to their absolute limits; they did not return to the barrack at each day's end in tears, crying about the awful conditions they had endured. The barrack was cleaner and lighter than the one at Birkenau had been, and Mira was surrounded by prisoners who had specialist jobs; 'those were elite people who were working for the Germans'. In Block 1, Mira found five women from home. Four of them acted in the role of *Stubenälteste*, in charge of cleaning and food distribution – Mira would become their helper – while the fifth, the *Blockälteste*, was an older woman called Marta. Coincidence would play a role here, too: Marta would reconnect with Josef from Spišská Stará Ves when the war was over, after he learned that his wife had been killed in concentration camp Bergen-Belsen. Marta and Josef married and rescued his daughter, the baby who had been taken in by Josef's neighbour. The couple raised his toddler as their own, and had a second girl together after the war.

* * *

Many of the women who Mira knew in Block 1 had been in various camps over the past two and a half years, and Block 1 felt like a relative haven for them all. At night, Mira slept on a mattress to herself, instead of sharing with several others, and often had 'easy' jobs: working in the kitchen and washing dishes, or dividing food into rations. She was not only able to take some tiny amounts of extra sustenance for herself, but could squirrel bits away for others, too.

Unfortunately, one day the *Lagerälteste* needed two women for a far more strenuous job, which involved dragging huge stones. It was difficult, exhausting and dusty, and Mira had had no idea exactly what it would entail. She wasn't to know that the SS did not always choose work to fit the prisoner; they often chose work to kill a prisoner. That certain prisoners should be annihilated through work – given tasks under cruel conditions that would hasten their deaths – was part of their genocidal policy.

Elza, a woman from a nearby town in Slovakia whom Mira first met in Block 1, refused to let her go. 'If Mira goes there, she is never coming back. That will be the end of her. She won't be able to make it. I am going to go instead.' And she did so. Twice. When she came back the first night, she was so weary she could barely speak, except to say, 'I don't think I have ever had a harder job.' Mira could never understand why Elza had made that sacrifice on her behalf.

In fact, all of the women fussed over her, treating her more like a much younger sister than a contemporary. Something about her tugged at their maternal instincts. Partly it was her age. They fretted about her and tried to make things easier for her. And they were grateful for her presence as well. When she arrived in Auschwitz I, she was like an alien from an exotic land: she could tell them how the world had looked long after they had been taken away, and her stories about the last few years made them feel like they were listening to magical fairytales from another universe. They needed to be transported elsewhere; their earlier days had been laced with atrocious, sickening smells because, as Mira said, 'The smell of the burned bodies carried far.'

At night, after they had all returned from their work, someone would say, 'Now, Mira – you sing!' She had a hauntingly lovely voice, and she would sing all the songs they remembered from home: Slovak, Yiddish and Hebrew tunes. She would sing to please them and herself; it made her feel like she was giving them something in return when they retreated into their nostalgic memories. Perhaps she did not fully realise that she was also giving them something integral to their survival: she was giving them hope.

Mira did her best to forward their kindness. When her friend Blanka managed to visit Block 1 occasionally, Mira handed her a bar of soap, some bread and fed her hot soup.

And so the women briefly lived within these small suburbs of decency, while hell roared all around them.

* * *

After my father died, my brother, Fred, was helping Mira with some banking. At this stage in her life, she depended on the income that came from a number of flats, investment properties she had owned for five decades. As she became sicker, Fred helped her manage the paperwork, but he was stopped short when he noticed an unusual repeated entry. My mother was paying out a sum every month, and Fred had never heard of the beneficiary. When he asked her about it, she had to confess: earlier that year, when she was interviewing prospective tenants for one of her unlet flats, she met a woman whose son had a disability. Mira's flat was unsuitable for their needs – it was far too small – but the woman could not afford anything larger. Mira made this stranger a promise: she would deposit some money into the woman's bank account each month for a year, to enable her to rent a bigger place.

Her actions seemed inexplicable, but when I learned about her experiences at Auschwitz, I understood this behaviour a little better. Sometimes, those who are weaker need help. If you are in a position to give it to them, it is incumbent upon you to do so.

* * *

Mira knew her situation could have been worse. Edit was given a severe punishment after a Polish political prisoner asked her to pass on a letter to another woman. She did not read it, nor ask what it was about. As Mira explained, 'She wasn't thinking very clearly. She only wanted to please someone; she did not think it could be dangerous.' As Edit hid the letter in her shoe, she did not realise she was being watched by a Ukrainian prisoner, spying for the SS. When she was caught with the letter in her possession – it turned out to be political in content – she was sent to Block 11.

Also known as Death Block, it was where prisoners were sent to be punished, tortured or executed. There was the 'death wall', against which prisoners were shot; cell 18, the 'starvation cell', where prisoners were left to die without food or water, and four 'standing cells', in which it was impossible to sit or lie down. Edit was likely placed in the so-called 'dungeon', a dark cell with a small, single window covered with a metal screen punched with air holes.

She always remembered the name of the man who brought her water to drink, and even lemons to suck when her throat was sore: Ya'akov Kozelczyk, the Jewish *Kapo* in charge. He had once handed her a tablet to swallow so that she could instigate her own death if she wished, in case she was about to hang. She would not need it. Miraculously, after several weeks, she ended up on a truck back to Birkenau. It was unclear how this came to pass; in her heart, she believed she had Ya'akov to thank.

In Block 11, inscriptions were scrawled everywhere. They were prisoners' last words, carved into the walls and windowsills with hairpins, fingernails, pencils. In one of those cells, Edit engraved her own name – Edit Rose – perhaps to ensure that she would not be so easily eradicated.

Twenty

Mira had arrived at Auschwitz II–Birkenau three months earlier. With Allied armies starting to close in on the concentration camps, the Nazis were frantically trying to move their prisoners to forced labour camps within Germany.

She left Auschwitz nine days before the Red Army arrived, on 18 January 1945. Two days prior, the prisoners learned that the storerooms would be packed up, the warehouses set on fire. Mira was among those prisoners who suddenly had access to the food pantries and clothing storage facilities.

From the kitchen, she took a loaf of bread and some cheese. Other prisoners latched onto the things they had been deprived of for so long: large cans of meat, as well as heavy jars of fruit conserves. But Mira thought about what she would be capable of carrying in her weakened condition, and also considered which foodstuffs would not spoil.

When she reached the clothing storeroom, Mira saw prisoners grabbing new uniforms because theirs were worn and torn. But Mira's was not. She looked around the room for something else, and immediately saw what she wanted: a pair of half-boots. Something her father used to say reverberated in her head. Since Spišská Stará Ves had always been so snowy and cold in winter, Dolfie had some sage advice. 'Even when it is cold outside, if your feet are warm and dry, you will be all right and you won't feel the cold so much.' That was Mira's thinking when she grabbed the shoes; she also helped herself to a coat to act as extra padding over her thin uniform.

She knew they would be travelling on foot. What she did not realise was that this walk would later be called a death march, dubbed thus because of how many people died while walking. Prisoners were forced to travel extremely long distances with little sustenance, while exposed to the freezing cold. If they could not keep up, or tried to run away, they were shot. They were shot even if all they wanted was to rest for a few minutes. Of the nearly sixty thousand prisoners – mainly Jewish – who left on death marches from Auschwitz, between nine and fifteen thousand would meet their end along the way.

* * *

The marches out of Auschwitz took place over a period of five days. Mira was among the group of women who left on 18 January. It was the middle of winter, and the temperature dropped to icy lows, plummeting to minus 20 degrees Celsius. The snow fell incessantly and the ground was wet with slush. To explain how cold it was would be to describe the way a person feels when they slip into ice water and then emerge – sodden, freezing, miserable. Imagine these withered women, so skinny that their bones looked ready to burst from beneath their skin, their collar bones protruding. Then imagine them so cold that the chill assaulted them like an enemy, vicious and strategic. It was a cold they could not stop thinking about, a cold that conspired to undo them. The cold alone made some of them long for death.

The falling snow served only one good purpose: when it melted, the prisoners could lick it off their clothes, quenching their terrible thirst a little. There was no respite from any of it: not the frigid conditions, not the pain, not the hunger, not the thirst. A girl fainted, and another woman begged a guard for a drink. His answer? The woman was shot, the girl left for dead.

At night, Mira slept in a barn with a small cohort of twenty, the floor covered in straw. It was not good to feel too complacent after having done everything during the day to survive; people died in the night, too, doing nothing. Nor was it uncommon for someone to fall asleep and wake in the morning to find their neighbour dead beside them. But even if the prisoners believed they were walking towards their deaths, many fought to stay strong in an act of standing up against the Nazis.

It was startling how the smallest of decisions could have such large ramifications. When most of the women went to open their food, they realised how disastrous their choices had been. Their big, heavy cans filled with meat had become too burdensome to carry, but once the cans were opened they knew that the contents would quickly become frozen and spoil. Then they remembered that Mira had chosen to bring bread and some of them made a deal with her. 'Mira, do you want some meat? Give me a piece of bread, and you can have some meat.' It was nothing much, just scraps. But this way, Mira managed to eat something that sustained her a little more, for a little longer.

She had made a similarly prescient choice by bringing along spare shoes, when some women didn't have even a single pair, and were forced to march in bare feet. At night, those who had shoes found that they were soaked through from the wet slush. Several decided to take them off and give their feet some respite overnight. Others kept them on. Both groups fared poorly. For the women who had taken off their shoes, they struggled to put them back on in the morning, as their feet had become swollen and their still-damp shoes had shrunk. The women who had slept in their shoes were equally uncomfortable, with the moisture opening blisters and causing their feet to ache. But Mira could take her shoes off and have a completely dry, fresh pair to wear the next day. Her extra shoes — especially the boots, which were far superior to the wooden or leather clogs that some prisoners wore, having been issued them in camp — helped her greatly on the arduous march.

There was no escaping terror, even on the open road. Mira heard the sound of several gunshots in the distance, and she knew what this meant. She never tried to see what had happened, or find out who had been killed. Occasionally she saw someone lagging behind before eventually moving out of line to sit by the side of the road, unable to continue walking. She knew what that meant, too. 'Many prisoners made it, but those who were not able to [walk] were killed. There was no other way. There were only two ways.'

By the third day, Mira saw many prisoners lying dead on the paths. She tried to shield her eyes as she passed them, looking at the road ahead. But there was one woman she could not help but look at. She must have been lying there for some time, as her stomach had swollen to shocking proportions, distended 'like a balloon'. It was a gruesome sight. 'You tried not to see, you tried to look forward. Self-preservation is a very important thing at a time like that,' she said. It was not just the appalling sight of a dead body, treated as waste matter, but the constant reminder: *This could be you next.*

When the women had to relieve themselves, they were able to move off the path and crouch behind trees, since their route took them through a forest. A friend of Mira's pulled her aside. 'Why don't we escape?' she whispered. 'We can run between the trees.' But Mira did not know where they were, or what kind of people lived in the nearby houses. She was too scared to escape, to risk her life. It was easy for her to imagine a bullet tearing through her back as she fled. 'I thought, Where will I run, [here] in Germany? So I didn't. Some girls did run, and survived that way.'

And some of those who stayed also survived, against all odds. Mira had made a friend in camp, Aliska Rosenblum, who as a *Stubenälteste* – the room elder - had been allowed to have an appendix operation three days before departure. It was not a show of Nazi goodwill; SS physicians occasionally practised their craft on prisoners. She was still recovering and could barely walk, so her friends took it in turns to carry her, pairs of them fashioning a makeshift seat with the flats of their hands for her to rest on. When she sat, she put her arms over the women's shoulders to try to relieve some of the weight on them. They did this for twenty or thirty minutes apiece and then swapped; occasionally Aliska hobbled along on her own. It is hard to imagine how they managed this; at the end of three days, the prisoners had covered somewhere between thirty-four and thirty-nine miles. Aliska made it all the way: not just through the war, but to a new life in Israel afterwards.

After their brutal, relentless march, the surviving prisoners were herded onto cattle trains. None of them knew where they would end up.

Twenty-one

It was night-time when the prisoners arrived at an aeroplane hangar that had been converted into a prison camp. They were now on German soil. It was freezing cold, the ground covered in thick snow, and the women had to stay inside the guarded area; they were not allowed to venture outside. Mira had one slice of bread remaining from the death march; she had carefully kept it aside in case there was a shortage of food at her next destination. When she went to sleep, she tucked the piece of bread under her neck to use as a pillow so nobody could steal it.

In the morning, the bread was gone; somebody had managed to take it without disturbing her. Lying on the straw, without food and unable to leave the hangar's confines, she felt desperate. But Mira once again remembered what her father had taught her: 'Help yourself and God will help you.' As she explained it, 'You can't lie on your back and cry that something is going to happen – you've got to do something … And I saw that something had to be done.'

Her solution was to approach the Jewish *Kapo* guarding the door. 'I have to go to the toilet,' Mira told her.

'No, no, no,' said the *Kapo*. 'You cannot go out. It's not allowed.'

'But I need to go very urgently,' Mira pleaded. She was so insistent that the *Kapo* finally gave in.

Walking around outside, she heard an *Aufseherin*, a female guard working in Nazi camps, calling out, 'Is anybody here from Kanada?' Mira did not even know what that meant. She knew the country of Canada but not the slang word in Holocaust terminology: it was the area of the camp in Auschwitz where the confiscated possessions of the prisoners were held. It was partly given this name because, like Canada, it was a place of great riches. It was also a sought-after job at the camp – women who were sent to this storage facility to sort out the items and send them back to Germany could also smuggle out extra rations or possessions while there.

Yet despite her ignorance, when Mira heard the guard ask, 'Is anyone from Kanada?' she quickly spoke up. She had nothing to lose. 'I am,' she said.

The guard ushered Mira, and ten others who had raised their hands, into a car and drove off.

When they stopped, they found themselves at a kitchen that prepared meals for the German SS. The cook, a German woman, took one look at the unkempt group and threw up her hands in dismay. '*Mein Gott!* I can't let you touch anything the way that you are! Here is hot water and a bucket – wash yourselves!'

Mira could hardly believe what was happening. 'Do you know what that meant?' she later said. 'It was like we had won the lottery. To have, after days of walking – suddenly to be offered hot water with soap and a towel to dry yourself? To be in a warm kitchen?'

They all cleaned themselves, and the cook fed them a hearty meal. It wasn't even necessary; the German SS officers left plenty of food on their plates to be scavenged afterwards. Mira was astounded. 'All we had to do was peel vegetables, wash the dishes, clean the sink – in a kitchen that was so beautiful and warm.'

There was one problem: when she returned to the hangar that night, she had lost the spot that she had slept in previously, and there was no longer any room for her to lie down. She walked around, searching for somewhere to rest, and finally found a narrow space next to two German Jewish women. She made a deal with them: if they saved her that place on the floor the following night, she would bring them food from the kitchen. It was an arrangement that pleased everyone, and Mira continued this way for almost a week. Every day, the cook gave the girls hot water for washing and plentiful food. The kitchen job would sustain her for the next part of her ordeal. She did not know then how greatly she would need that preparation.

* * *

I would never have dared throw out leftover bread when I was young. Although in certain regards my mother was not like many Holocaust survivors – she did not stockpile tins of non-perishable items in her pantry, for instance – she was adamant that food never be wasted and bread never be discarded. Occasionally, when the family did not finish the pair of challah loaves from Shabbat, I would watch the bread deteriorate: the crust losing its egg-gloss finish, the inside crumb becoming harder and staler. Once it became too unpleasant to toast, my mother would cut the bits up into small pieces, browning them in the oven to make croutons. Or else she would soften them again with some water, and toss bits to the birds that gathered in front of her house. A piece of bread accidentally put into the rubbish bin would have infuriated her.

If she caught sight of any of her children walking around the house wearing only socks and no shoes, she would be similarly angry. That was because when a person is sitting shiva – the seven-day mourning period observed after a family member's death – Jewish law dictates that leather shoes cannot be worn, and stockinged feet are reminiscent of the despair the mourner is experiencing. My mother did not want to bring death to her door in any way; she had seen so much of it. Mimicking those rituals was to disrespect their underlying meaning.

But that wasn't to say that everything boomeranged back to the Holocaust for her. It was not like that at all. I remember crying to her about a perceived hurt, now so small that I cannot think of what it was. She put her arms around my shoulders and rocked me. Midway through crying, I had a sense of how petty my sadness might appear to her, and I suddenly stopped. 'How can you stand it?' I asked her. 'How can you bear it when I am this upset about something so small, after you have gone through so much?' She did not even have to think about her answer. 'Pain is pain,' she said. 'What you go through is hard for you. What I went through was hard for me.' I never forgot her capacity for empathy, and I was never so aware of its expansiveness as in that moment.

Twenty-two

Another move, another train, atrocious conditions. Death from suffocation, extreme thirst, exhaustion or being crushed: who knew there were so many ways for people to die en route? The prisoners had come to Ravensbrück, a concentration camp in Germany, around fifty miles north of Berlin, which had been built for female prisoners in 1938. It was used as a place of execution, and countless women were shot dead – literally countless: records were not kept, and so the number is unknown. In January 1945, a temporary gas chamber was erected.

When Mira arrived, Ravensbrück was horribly over-crowded, which made for deplorable sanitary conditions and helped foster a typhus epidemic. In January 1945, there were more than fifty thousand prisoners in the camp, mainly female. Mira knew they were only in transit there, and she could not wait to leave. 'It was an awful place,' she said. 'There was not much food – some watery soup, or something like that – but there it was only hunger that I knew. It was very cold and very dirty. There were lice everywhere.' In fact, lice had infiltrated the camp in plague proportions, and there were so many prisoners packed in together that four women slept on a single bed, with no blankets to cover themselves. Everyone felt like they were on their own. It was disorganised, chaotic, nightmarish. 'It was such a terrible camp. It was stinking. The air was stinking. The rooms were stinking. The atmosphere there: you were pushed, you were not given [anything] to eat, you were treated like … I can't explain, it was really terrible.'

Once, during the day, she decided to step outside of her barrack. Standing in the fresh air, a woman ran past her block, frantic. She shouted to Mira, '*Uciekaj! Uciekaj! Polują na króliki.*' '*Run away, run away, they are hunting for rabbits.*'

Mira understood some Polish – she had picked it up from the Polish prisoners in camp – so she knew the literal translation of the words, but had no idea what they meant. *Why should I hide when they're only looking for rabbits?* she wondered. Still, she had heard the terror in the woman's voice, so she ran. *Run, hide, run, hide.* She hid behind the barrack before slipping back inside when all was clear.

She later found out that Ravensbrück was famous for its medical experiments; on that day, whoever was standing outside was rounded up and collected for that purpose. It was impossible to guess what she might have been subjected to. The experiments started in Ravensbrück in 1942. Incisions were made into some prisoners' legs and contaminated substances then injected into them so that an infection would form. Others had their bones deliberately broken. In the officials' attempt to discover how to better treat injured German soldiers, some of these experiments involved the amputation of a healthy limb. Syphilis was injected into women's spinal cords. Many women would die from these procedures; others were left with lifelong damage. The latter group would return to their barracks in a mutilated state, and they became known among the prisoners as *die Kaninchen*, 'rabbits', because from then on they could no longer walk, only hop.

Articulate as she was, Mira would always grasp for words when describing Ravensbrück, repeating some adjectives ('awful') often, or elongating others ('te-rri-ble') for effect. It was through her stumbling that she conveyed the bleakness and horror of that camp. It was clear that not even the precision of language could capture it.

Mira was in Ravensbrück for less than a week. She did not think she would have been able to stand it there much longer.

Twenty-three

It was February 1945. The prisoners had all endured more than five years of wartime, with some having spent years in concentration camps. Each one of them was physically exhausted, malnourished, gaunt. But they had also lost much of their spirit. So many felt defeated, hopeless, despairing.

The women were again put into different groups, sent off in different directions. Mira arrived at what would be her fourth and final concentration camp: Neustadt–Glewe, named for the nearby town in Germany. It was a satellite camp of Ravensbrück, and very small: it had only been established in September 1944, and Mira was one of around five thousand prisoners, mainly female, in a camp built for nine hundred.

When it came time for work assignments, and Mira learned there was a factory that dealt in aircraft parts production, she volunteered to once more toil in the fields instead. She had never forgotten Blanka's experience of working in the factory in Auschwitz, and she knew she did not have the strength for that. On her first day, she walked with a group of prisoners to the fields, a route which took them through the back of several farmhouses. Behind one, they happened upon a large oil drum, around a metre tall, with a fire blazing within. The appetising smell filled their nostrils long before they drew close enough to see where it came from: resting above the drum was a mound of potatoes still in their skins, baking in the flames.

Accompanying the prisoners was a member of the Wehrmacht. So many of his ilk were later found guilty of committing systematic war crimes, but this particular soldier displayed a show of humanity. Mira believed he had known the drum was present before they arrived, even though he acted surprised and said, 'Oh? Potatoes! Here! You can take some!' The women reached in, each grabbing a whole potato. Mira said a silent prayer of thanks to the German residents who owned those little farmhouses; they must have been aware that this was a route for prisoners and had left the food there deliberately. There were fresh potatoes again the next day, and the day after that. It was a simple act of kindness that buoyed her spirits.

But not for long. Every day the prisoners still had to stand at the *Appellplatz* for the roll call, which would stretch out interminably. Even worse, Mira dreaded the cruel SS officer who hovered around while it took place, bringing his vicious German shepherd with him. To amuse himself, he would command the dog to attack the women while they were standing in their rows. Sometimes the dog would only growl or bark, baring its teeth, but periodically it would bite. Everyone was scared of it and its unpredictability, and all the prisoners tried to avoid standing in the front row, where the dog and owner most often frequented. But even that strategy failed occasionally: if the SS officer saw the women congregating at the rear, he would travel to the back row, letting his dog loose there instead. 'It was very, very scary. It was a very frightening camp,' said Mira.

* * *

One month passed, then two. Mira continued to work in the fields, but as the days wore on, her body weakened. Rations were unreliable, so there was little to eat. Even though winter had turned to early spring, she was always very cold and soon suffered from the effects of starvation, overwork and no proper sleeping or hygiene facilities. But worst of all, some of her light had gone out. Her sunny demeanour felt like it belonged to a long-ago time. She lost weight steadily. 'Suddenly, my strength went. It was a very bad camp, and I deteriorated there very, very much,' she said. In the time she was there, one-fifth of the camp population would die, mainly from disease and starvation.

Like her brother Yanchi, she had become a *Muselmann*. Her body was withered, skeletal, a shadow of a body.

The term also indicated something about that person's desire to live. They often possessed no will at all: not to move, not to eat, not to care. What was the point? Those prisoners who continued to feel something only continued to suffer. The *Muselmänner* had found another route out, but they did not typically survive long. When a prisoner looked this way, they were shot, gassed or put to death by another method. Even this close to the war's end, sick prisoners who were no longer capable of working at Neustadt-Glewe were usually returned to Ravensbrück to be killed. Somehow, Mira escaped being transferred. But she was no longer able to turn up for the *Appellplatz*, and the other women would cover for her, calling out her name at roll call, and trying to ensure that the guards would not realise she was missing from her work.

By April, she had barely eaten proper food for three months. Her body was giving out. Pus-filled abscesses formed on her gums, and her teeth grew loose, wobbling when she touched them. She could no longer eat hard food, and was unable to eat on her own. She would simply lie on the floor of the barrack, where there was not even a bunk bed for some relief.

The girl who slept next to her – a sweet, German Jewish teenager – cared for her as best she could. Most days, she brought rations to Mira's side, and fed her slowly. She would talk to Mira, telling stories about her home and detailing the shop her parents had owned. Mira listened, but could not respond. 'If some girls brought me a little bit of soup, I drank. If they didn't, I didn't care. At that stage, you don't feel hunger. You don't care about food, you don't care about getting up – nothing.'

Days ticked past, and Mira longed for it all to be over. She knew her body was ready to stop. It had come to the end. All that had been keeping her alive was her willpower. But now her reserves were exhausted. She still believed in God, and she still believed in an afterlife. The afterlife was now far more appealing. She longed to be reunited with her parents. She was not sure if her sister or any of her brothers were still alive, but there was every chance they were dead as well.

One night, late in April, Mira decided to pray. She said the *Shema*, the prayer she always said before going to sleep. She recited the Hebrew words with her right hand covering her eyes, as is prescribed, in order to separate the physical world from the spiritual one. '*Shema Yisrael, Adonai Eloheinu, Adonai echad.*' Hear, O Israel, the Lord is our God, the Lord is One. She added a silent prayer of her own. *Please, God, I am ready to die. Please take me to be with my family again.* She felt so close to death that she had no doubt: this would be the last night she saw the stars, and there would be no more mornings in this realm for her to endure.

* * *

She was dreaming about her mother. This dream was distinctive, uniquely vivid. She was back at her childhood home in Spišská Stará Ves. Genya, who seemed to know the ordeals her daughter had faced, appeared by her side. In her hand, a warm bowl of soup. Mira felt weak, so Genya fed her the broth, spoonful by spoonful. Then Genya held her tight: '*Meine Mira-le*, it will be all right, it will be all right.' She soothed her daughter, and whispered something in her ear. Through the cobwebs of her dream, Mira felt the tingle of Genya's breath. She reached out to her mother, for the softness of her mother's arms. She would never have to leave this space. She was finally safe, after so long …

When Mira woke up on the barrack floor the next morning, she was stunned. First, it was hard to believe that she had lived through the night. But another thing: although she had dreamed about her mother frequently in camp, this dream had been singularly realistic. She was surprised to feel revived, her belly not so hungry – as if her mother really *had* somehow come and fed her soup. In her heart, Mira did not believe this was just a dream. She was certain that Genya had managed to cross the threshold between life and death to be with her daughter, to help her. And she remembered what Genya whispered to her at the end: 'Mira, stay alive until your birthday. Stay alive until then. On your birthday, I will come and save you.'

Mira had no idea how that could be possible; she had been in four camps for close to eight months, and she could not see a way out. But she had sufficient faith in the dream, and enough trust in her mother, to make a vow to herself. Her birthday was only four days away. She did not have much energy left, but her mother's visit had given her some *koach*, some strength. She could hang on until then. And if that day came and went and nothing happened, she would allow herself to die, once and for all. She was sure that, next time, her body would listen.

So, she willed herself to live. And on that fourth day, everything changed. Her captors and tormentors – hearing that the prisoners at nearby Ravensbrück had been liberated – fled Neustadt-Glewe overnight. It took place in the late hours of 30 April 1945. Mira Blumenstock's eighteenth birthday.

Twenty-four

Mira had gone to sleep on the eve of her birthday and was woken the next morning by the sound of women shouting. She opened her eyes to see two of her friends running around, yelling something beyond belief: 'Girls! The Germans are gone! There are no Germans! The doors are open! It's finished!' Under the cover of darkness, the Nazis had bolted. The Camp of Corpses, as some had called it, was no more.

The first thing any of them could think about was food. But her two friends were paralysed with fear. Although they knew where the kitchen and its supplies were, they did not want to leave the safety of their barrack. They were too scared to walk out the door and investigate.

Still so fragile and weak, Mira never understood how she managed to stand on her feet. 'Just the knowledge that you could leave gave me strength. By some miracle, I got up. And I told them both that I would go to the kitchen.'

She hobbled along, slowly but steadily. When she reached the kitchen, she saw prisoners raiding the supplies, as expected.

But lurking in the doorway was a non-Jewish gang of females, pouncing on some of those who exited, nabbing their food. It clearly was a more efficient way for them to gather supplies, saving them the effort of searching for tins themselves.

Mira realised she was no match for these intimidating women, but she had an idea. Noting that they were only interested in large quantities of food, and being too sickly to carry a heavy load anyway, she collected just a scant amount – a tiny piece of bread, one small serve of conserves – so that the gang would leave her alone when they saw her paltry stash. 'They did not attack me, because for one sardine, they were not interested,' said Mira, who walked past them easily, taking the items to her friends at the barrack for safeguarding. She returned to the kitchen several more times, until the trio had enough food to share. They sat on the floor together, eating slowly so that they would not get sick. Their bodies had become so unaccustomed to adequate servings of food; they instinctively knew that eating too much, or too quickly, would kill them.

None of them wanted to stay in the filthy barracks, where there were only the uncomfortable, dirty bunks to sleep on. But where would they go? On the outskirts of the camp were the former lodgings of the female guards. Mira joined a small group who were prepared to investigate, around half-a-dozen in all. Naturally, the rooms had been abandoned, and appeared like a sanctuary to these women when they opened one door: the room was spacious and clean, with two soft beds and white sheets. They had all forgotten what that kind of luxury looked like, and decided to stay the night.

Everyone settled in, but Mira felt uneasy: the first thing she noticed was that the door had no lock on it. She made a suggestion to the others, nodding to the large wooden wardrobe that stood in the room. 'Let's push this in front of the door,' she said. The others weren't convinced. 'Who is going to come in?' one asked. Mira shrugged, but insisted nevertheless. 'I don't know why I said that. But I said it, and they listened.' It took all of them to move the heavy piece of furniture into place.

* * *

For some Holocaust survivors, liberation marked their first encounter with people who acted humanely. Some prisoners would see their liberators as their saviours, connecting with them immediately, and being treated with tenderness and respect in response. But not all forces that entered the camp for the first time since Nazi occupation were compassionate, or able to offer adequate help. Some were unprepared for what they came across, and their shock and bewilderment would immobilise or traumatise them. They would see the starved prisoners, the bodies discarded like junk, and vomit or cry. Others were repulsed, and barely saw the ex-prisoners as human. And there were those who furthered the trauma, so that even liberation became another obstacle to survive.

In the middle of the night, suddenly: a tremendous ruckus. Loud banging on their door. To Mira, it filled her ears like a gunshot. *Boom. Boom. Boom.* Russian words, fierce and demanding: '*Otkroy dverh!*' Mira understood enough Russian – it was a Slavic language, like her mother tongue – to know what was being said: 'Open the door!' She put her finger to her lips to hush the other girls. They all huddled closely together, staying silent, terrified. They could hear the rough jiggling of their door handle from the other side, someone trying to force the door open. But it was impossible; the wardrobe prevented it from budging. Sounds of several pairs of footsteps moving on to the room next door. Then, women's screams, shocked, scared.

Mira's group quickly ascertained what was happening: Russian soldiers – who had come to the camp to liberate it in the early hours of 2 May – had broken into the room next to theirs. Mira never caught sight of them, so did not know who the room's occupants were until she heard the muffled cries, the pleading, the terror.

A girl's voice, screaming in Polish: '*Mamusia! Ratunku!*' Mummy! Help me!

The woman, replying: 'What can I do, my darling? Don't cry. It will pass. I can't help you.' And later, her pleas became more urgent. 'Daughter! Survive, survive!'

Of all the ways Mira had imagined her first night of freedom, it was not listening to the wretched cries of a mother and daughter being raped, while she tried not to make a sound next door.

Twenty-five

The following morning, Mira could not bear the thought of staying in the camp's grounds any longer. The women had another idea: in the town of Neustadt-Glewe, after which the camp had been named, there were many abandoned houses. In these, prisoners could find much-needed food, clothing and other necessities – as well as somewhere to sleep.

Even after just one day of liberation, Mira started to feel physically improved from the food she had eaten. After walking into the village, her group stumbled upon a small house, its doors open. It was tidy inside, and there was a decent pantry. The women washed, and used the stove to prepare some food, their first proper hot meal in so long. They were in the kitchen when a Russian soldier wandered in, surprising them all. He acted like he was an expected guest who had arrived a little early for dinner. 'Oh, how nice!' he exclaimed. 'Can I have some of that food?' Awkwardly, Mira handed him a plate. She was the only one who could understand what he was saying; the rest of them, being German, could not.

She was alone with him in the lounge room, when he leaned in close to her. 'You know what would be nice?' he asked. 'It would be nice for us to go into the bedroom.'

After her terrifying experience the night before, she knew what that meant. And she had also learned that her liberators were capable of violence and unpredictability. If he was going to wrestle her – in her underweight and fragile state – she knew who would win.

But despite being weak, she had not lost her ability to think quickly. Although bile rose up to her throat and her heart started beating rapidly, she responded in kind. 'I think so too,' she said coquettishly. 'You wait here. I am going to send the other girls away.'

'*Horosho*,' he said. 'Good.' And he sat back in his chair as she walked into the next room.

Closing the door behind her, she joined the others in the kitchen. There was no time to explain. 'Girls, run!'

They all bolted out of the back entrance, hurrying back to their barrack at camp. In only a couple of days, Mira had learned a sobering lesson. 'I saw that there was nowhere that you could be safe,' she said.

* * *

When she had been in the camp at Neustadt-Glewe, Mira often encountered a familiar face: Libush Korn, a friend of her sister, Olga. The two had travelled on the same route together since Auschwitz, yet despite their shared history, they were eleven years apart in age and did not naturally gravitate to one another. Still, when Mira was trying to decide where to go next, she approached Libush, asking what her plans were.

Libush had become close with a Yugoslav woman in camp, imprisoned for being Communist. She explained to Mira that this friend had invited her to join her group. They planned to search for a larger town, hoping that help would be available there. A horse and cart had been organised; the cart would carry the luggage, while the group walked alongside it.

'Can I walk with you?' Mira asked.

Libush was unsure. Her own connection to the Yugoslav women was tenuous – she was the only Jewish one in that crowd – but she asked Mira to appear before the group that evening and present her case.

When Mira turned up, the group were unequivocal in their response. 'No, we can't take anyone else. There is no more room on the cart.'

Mira refused to give up; she tried a different tack. 'What do I have to do with the cart? I don't have anything, just one little case,' she said. It was a small bag – not much bigger than a handbag – that she had found in the empty house, together with its contents: a pair of underwear, a single blouse, socks, a pair of shoes and a small amount of food. 'I can walk behind you. I can carry my own bag.'

She could hear them grumbling, but they acquiesced; if this scrawny girl wanted to walk behind them, out of their sight, she could. It was a free world.

Leaving the concentration camp, after so many torturous months, should have been a cause for celebration. But as she started walking, still so gaunt and undernourished, Mira realised she was more alone than ever. Her father Dolfie's words – every man for himself – had never felt truer.

Twenty-six

And so they walked. The horse and cart in front with ten women at the rear, and Mira behind them, trying to be inconspicuous. She could hear the lively chatter ahead but was not a part of it, and so tried to concentrate on her steps, the road and what lay ahead. She was philosophical about her lot. *At least I have someone to follow,* she said to herself.

They continued in this manner for three days. All along the way, villages were dotted with uninhabited houses and deserted farms, and every evening, when it was time to rest, the group chose the nearest one to stay in. They would find a chicken roaming the yard and kill it, then celebrate their newfound freedom together over a hearty dinner. But they never invited Mira to join them nor inquired how she was faring. 'They did not ask me, "Do you want something to eat?" and I did not ask them for any food. I always had something that was enough for me there, still in my bag. I had my piece of bread, and some milk. They ignored me; absolutely, I didn't exist.' She sat separately and at some distance, even from Libush, who perhaps worried about her own standing with the other women.

On the third day, they chanced upon another group of ex-prisoners – a dozen young Czech men their age, half of them Jewish. Immediately, there was a conviviality among the throng, the women laughing at whatever the young men said. Eventually one of the women piped up. 'Why don't we join up and walk together?' The men, who were heading towards Czechoslovakia, agreed.

Mira took her position behind the others, and that night, when everyone was eating and conversing, she again sat apart from the group, nibbling at whatever scraps she had managed to secure. She barely felt hungry anyway; her stomach was still so shrunken.

One of the non-Jewish men saw her there, and turned to address the rest. 'What's happening with her? Why isn't she eating with us?' he asked, nodding in Mira's direction.

Mira looked at the ground, pretending not to hear.

'Ach, she's not with us, she is only following us,' one woman replied.

The young man was confused. 'What do you mean? Is she also a prisoner from the camps?'

'Yes.'

'Did she do something wrong in camp? Is that why she is sitting over there?'

'No, she didn't do anything wrong, but she doesn't belong with us. She is not in our group.'

A moment earlier, the young man had been chatting to his friends, smiling broadly. Now he rose to his feet, standing tall. He spoke slowly and firmly and there was no mistaking the anger in his voice. His stance, his strength, put a sudden stop to the evening. 'How can you do that?' he demanded. 'She was a prisoner in camp, the same as you. You have got food here. We are going towards freedom, and this is how you treat her?' He went over to fetch Mira and bring her to the group. He continued to be attentive to her for the remainder of the meal.

'The girls were not very happy after that,' recalled Mira, 'but he was like my guardian angel.'

* * *

The next day, Mira resumed her position at the back. But the long days of walking had taken their toll on her, and she was lagging further and further behind. 'My forces started to be very, very weak,' she said. When the Czech man noticed, he ambled to her side. 'I can't walk very well anymore, and I can only go very slowly,' she told him. 'Don't worry. I will follow you and catch up.'

He immediately called out to the driver. 'Stop the cart!' When the driver didn't hear, he said it again, shouting this time. 'Stop the cart!'

As everyone came to a halt he made a loud announcement. 'Mira can't walk anymore and she cannot keep up. She is going to sit on top of the cart.'

The women howled in protest. Mira said, 'You have never heard screams of rage like that. "What? She is going to be sitting while we will be walking?" The racket that those girls made, you have no idea.'

'We are all tired!' the women countered, but the young man was insistent.

'You are tired, but she is *done*. She will not survive. She is going to sit there without you complaining, or all of us boys are going to leave you and go our separate ways.'

That was enough to end the argument. From then on, Mira sat on the cart, and her new friend made sure she ate some food, even when she did not feel like doing so.

Soon, authorities halted the mass of pedestrians – not just Mira's group, but everyone trying to leave Germany on foot. They were blocking the roads, making it impossible for cars to pass, and they were ordered to immediately find a place to stay until they were given further instructions.

* * *

They landed at a farmstead, far grander and more elaborate than anywhere else they had stayed; it must have once belonged to a very wealthy family. It had an upstairs level, and was completely deserted – or so they all thought, until someone went into the attic and was shocked to find an old German lady in her eighties lying there alone. It turned out that, because she had a disability, her family had left her there to rest, returning daily to feed her meals and wash her. Another room proved also to be occupied: by a commander in the Russian army, along with an officer who served under him. Mira described the commander as 'very intelligent' and felt safer with him there.

There was plenty of space for Mira's group: a large bedroom upstairs for the men, and one on the same level for the women. They had heard that people were congregating at meeting points in the city centre to find out when buses might be departing to their home towns in Czechoslovakia, Yugoslavia, Belgium. But progress was slow, and the group thought that the farmhouse would offer peaceful surrounds while they waited a few days for news. It was a brief halcyon period for them all: no work, no walking; just recovery and rest.

Some days later a declaration was made. World War II had officially ended.

It was 8 May 1945: Victory in Europe Day, also known as VE Day.

The Russian commander returned to the farmhouse in high spirits, and addressed the group. 'My officer and I will be hosting an evening to celebrate the end of the war, and I would like to invite two of the girls to join us.' He assured them all that his intentions were honourable, but he had one specific request. 'I heard that there is a girl here named Mira. Mira is like the Russian name Mir, and *mir* means peace in my language. Another girl is welcome to join, but I would ask that Mira is included in the pair.'

Mira was nervous, but did not feel that she had much choice. She tried to convince herself that they would not feel any attraction towards her. 'There was not much to look at, with me, because my head was shaved, I was skinny, and I looked like a real *Muselmann* in those times. But I still was scared.'

That evening, she and another young woman entered the sitting room where the men were hosting their celebration. When they opened the door, they saw a lace cloth-covered table laden with drinks, biscuits and other sought-after morsels. To Mira, it seemed like an incomparable feast. The officer moved to pour her a glass of whisky. Immediately, the commander intervened. 'No, no,' he said. 'She is too young for that, you cannot give it to her. She will have some orange juice.' Mira looked at him gratefully. The woman who had accompanied her was happily imbibing the alcohol, becoming increasingly loud and laughing merrily.

They all sat around the table and began to sing Russian and Slovak songs from home. Mira's voice rang out clearly and movingly, and the men listened to her appreciatively, their eyes glistening.

After an hour, the commander got to his feet. 'Thank you very much for coming,' he said to Mira and her friend politely.

She left, marvelling at what a delightful evening she had enjoyed.

* * *

Together, the commander and officer protected those in the house. Occasionally members of the Russians' troop visited, but their superiors made sure that everyone was respectful, especially to the females present. One of the soldiers had begun flirting with a Yugoslav woman in Mira's group, a Communist with whom he felt a like-mindedness. He even presented her with a gold necklace that she immediately flaunted. Mira said cryptically, 'They had an arrangement between them.'

The commander and officer were often away overnight, and during one of these absences, when the women were already asleep in their beds, the Russian soldier suddenly barged into the bedroom. In the darkness, he began lifting up the women's blankets, trying to find his lover, who had distinctively thick legs. When he found her, he asked her to join him in a room where they might have more privacy, and she agreed. A second soldier, a companion of the first, began groping the other women, indicating that he too wanted a dalliance.

By then, every woman in that bedroom had risen to her feet and begun shrieking. The young men – who slept on the same floor – were woken by the racket and raced in. The two Russian men absconded to another part of the house, while Mira and her group fled outside. The rude invasion had disturbed all of them, and no one felt safe indoors any longer. They decided they would find another place to sleep for the night, quickly settling on a peasant's barn nearby. They knew that the commander would return in the morning to restore calm and security to their residence once more.

But when they returned to the farmstead the next day, the house was eerily quiet. Mira had a sense of foreboding as soon as she walked through the entrance: inside, doors had been flung open, furniture seemed askew. At first the house appeared abandoned, until they came upon one of the unused bedrooms. The door was shut, and when they tried to turn the knob, they discovered it locked. They banged on it, and shouted, but there was no movement on the other side that they could hear. Two of the men threw themselves against the wood, trying to force it open. Eventually, they broke it down.

Inside, the young Yugoslav woman was lying there, unconscious. She was in a terrible state: naked, bruised, battered. The village doctor was located, and confirmed what they all suspected: she had been raped multiple times. The doctor said he had never encountered an assault as brutal.

However, that was not the only crime that had taken place. When the group went to check on the other inhabitant, the elderly woman in the attic, they found her distraught, inconsolable. The second soldier, having failed to find a girl for himself, had raped the old woman.

'What did he want from me? What did he want from me?' she kept repeating, over and over again.

Gradually, the Yugoslav woman's cuts and bruises healed, but she had clearly changed in other ways. 'She was very, very mentally distressed after that. She never recovered,' said Mira.

The two soldiers paid for their heinous acts. When the commander returned the next day, he ordered that both men be shot and killed. It was the first time since the war had begun that Mira learned that somebody could be held accountable – and punished – for their actions.

* * *

My mother told this story to me when she had surpassed the age of that old lady by quite a number of years, and she had also revealed it in official testimonies that were videotaped many decades after the war. In one recounting, I could see how hard it was for her to press the words forward, as if each syllable was sticking in her throat, nauseating her. She appeared clearly shaken by the memory. But another time, she told the same story in a rather bizarre manner, almost as if it were an anecdote she was setting up that had a punchline at the end.

The only way I could make sense of this latter approach was to remember a genetic trait: my sister Lilianne and I are prone to laughing when we hear that something terrible has occurred. It is not that we think it is funny; it is more like a nervous reaction, an emotional switch gone haywire. Maybe it is a protective device as well, learned from our mother.

When it came to relaying her Holocaust experiences, Mira could be matter-of-fact, conveying the events plainly. Not quite without emotion, but also not overcome by those feelings. 'I am one of the very few, I suppose, who even now do not have bad dreams about camps, and don't remember those things. I was able to wipe it off my mind,' she told me.

Sometimes I wondered how much Mira left out. For instance, she never spoke about the hanging of Roza Robota to me directly; I had only heard about it by watching one of her testimonies, although she repeated it another time in an address at my children's Jewish school. I was not sure if I would ever know the entirety of her story. There might have been some things she chose not to elaborate on, some details that memory had buried, and others that she herself had kept hidden, prioritising her own sanity over the record.

And did those memories get worse as time went on, like a festering wound that was never able to completely heal? Or maybe the scar tissue had become so thick and impenetrable that what lay underneath could no longer hurt her. Certainly, there were times that she spoke about incidents in a way that was almost neutral, as if she had learned the trick of bearing witness without reliving its pain.

I knew that for many survivors, some memories eventually became too hard to suppress. I had once visited a Jewish aged-care facility in Melbourne and learned about a problem unique to that institution: a good portion of residents there were Holocaust survivors, and as they got older and their minds muddled, they were less able to cope. Elderly people who once had no trouble bathing would cry and scream when it came time to wash, remembering the gas chambers camouflaged as showers. It proved difficult for the carers, who were forced to find creative ways to help their charges stay clean.

The litany of my mother's horror stories, one after the other — so relentless and savage and inhuman — was hard to reconcile in the context of her entire life. 'How did you go on?' I asked her in her final months. 'How did you stop yourself from collapsing into a heap because of all that had happened?' And she said, emphasising every word clearly so that I never forgot them: 'I knew that that was in my past, and I had a future to live.'

Twenty-seven

There was no going back to the farmstead; the commander insisted they move, saying that the group needed the protection of supervised accommodation. They all wanted to be closer to the bus depot. Mira found refuge at a former prisoner-of-war camp which had become a Displaced Persons Camp, housing and repatriating those who were waiting to leave Germany for their countries of origin. The barracks were decent and clean, and Mira stayed in a room together with half-a-dozen other women.

But something had happened to Mira. Instead of getting better and stronger each day, as most others were doing, she was getting weaker and more fatigued. She lay in bed all day, her head spinning, unable to lift her head from the pillow. She did not complain. She did not say she was feeling poorly. She just gave in to her body and its collapse. She did not know it then, but tens of thousands of Holocaust survivors would die after liberation in a similar situation, having suffered from starvation and disease for so long.

One of her roommates had formed a romantic attachment to a Belgian major; he was not staying at the compound, but he visited her frequently. He was in his fifties and, to Mira, seemed an old man. She had no interest in anything going on around her. She ignored him. She ignored everything.

But the major took notice of her. 'What is happening with that girl?' he asked one day. 'Whenever I come, whether it is morning, evening or lunchtime, she is always asleep. What is wrong with her?'

The others dismissed his concerns. 'We don't know. Maybe she just likes to sleep.'

He was not so easily brushed off. He approached Mira's bed and sat on its edge. He gently shook her shoulders, and she stirred a little. 'Would you like to go for a walk?' he asked.

'I can't,' Mira replied. 'I am dizzy when I get up.'

The major asked if she had eaten; she said she had not. He asked her a few more questions, trying to determine her state of health. 'I will come back tomorrow,' he said, 'and I will take you to see a doctor.'

He was as good as his word. The next day he took Mira to a French doctor who had been treating the POWs. A physical examination showed that she was severely malnourished. As a first step, the doctor said, Mira must consume nutritious food that was high in vitamin A, such as liver. 'Otherwise, she is not going to last very long.'

There was no liver in the barracks, of course. But the officer had a solution, corralling the others in her room. 'I am coming back this evening with liver,' he said. 'No one else is allowed to eat it. If it is gone from the fridge here, you will have to deal with me.' He asked them to cook the liver, and returned that night to feed it to Mira himself, mouthful by mouthful. He did this twice again the next day, insisting also that she go for a walk with him – 'whether you want to or not' – even if just for a few steps. This continued in the same manner every day, and by the time a week had passed she could get out of bed easily, go for a short walk and feed herself.

Mira was puzzled by the major's interest in her. He was still involved with the other woman and his manner towards Mira was strictly avuncular, yet he had clearly made her health a priority. 'Why are you so good to me?' she asked him in German, the language in which they communicated.

Smiling, he stroked her cheek with the back of his hand. 'My dear,' he said, 'I have a daughter around your age. When I am doing this for you, I always think of her. I hope when I was in the war and far from home, that there was somebody who could give her help when she needed it.'

Mira's own father, Dolfie, was dead, and so was her mother. But here was a stranger who was displaying the purest act of parental kindness she could ever imagine.

* * *

Half a century after the Holocaust, Mira gave her first video testimony about what had occurred so that her account could be catalogued and kept forever: locally, in the Melbourne Holocaust Museum, but also overseas, at the United States Holocaust Memorial Museum in Washington, DC. Details about her family would additionally live on in Yad Vashem, the World Holocaust Remembrance Center, in Jerusalem, Israel.

For hours, Mira spoke of the terrible things she had been through. The murder of her father. Of her mother. Of Olga, her sister. Of her brother Yanchi. The things she had seen: cruelty and shootings and hangings and sadism and rape. At the end, the interviewer asked one final question. 'What do you think was the main thing that saved you?'

Mira did not have to think twice about her answer. 'The goodness of people,' she replied. She had said it to me before: 'In the Holocaust, I learned about the goodness of people.' It was the one thing she held aloft, intact. Rather than zeroing in on the people who had tried to destroy her, she focused on those who had helped her, and there were many, Jewish and non-Jewish alike: the Blumenstocks' *arizátor*, Julius Scholcz. Erich, the *Kapo* at Plaszow. Edit Rose, who had her transferred to Auschwitz I. Elza, who twice went for work detail there in her stead. The young Czech man who insisted she ride on the cart. The Russian commander. The Belgian major. And so many more, including even the SS officer who ordered her off the truck that drove her mother to her execution. Some of these people had risked their own lives to help her. Those were the people she thought about when the day's light grew dim. Those were the people worth remembering.

Twenty-eight

Finally, a bus going to Prague. Mira had never been there, but being back in Czechoslovakia felt like home. First, she was taken to a temporary hotel for a quarantine period, while doctors performed thorough check-ups and ensured that the former prisoners were free from disease. During that time, she had a visit from her 'guardian angel', the young Czech man who had stood up for her when she was trailing the cart in Germany. His home town was Prague, and he had kept track of Mira. He brought with him a cake his mother had baked. 'He was definitely in love with me,' Mira said, looking back. 'But at the time he did not say anything, and I did not know anything.'

After quarantine was completed, she was allowed to travel wherever she wanted – by train or bus – for free. In Prague, people were exchanging information with urgency: hundreds of people stood at the bus depot, calling out the names of their families and trying to learn their fate. Mira called out, 'Blumenstock family! Blumenstock family!' A man raised his hand. 'Yes! Your brothers Heshek and Shani are living in Košice, and your Aunt Roza Storch is in Kežmarok!' It was more than Mira had hoped for, and she was aware of her good fortune; so many other people around her had called out their family names only to be met with silence.

She decided to first go to her aunt, who lived in a town she knew well. On the train, Mira settled in for the trip, sitting opposite a young man. Halfway through, he leaned over to her. 'Excuse me, miss, but I have to ask you something. I am fascinated. Whenever I look at you, you are either eating or sleeping, but nothing else. Where have you been?' The tattooed number on Mira's arm was covered by her sleeve, her shorn hair was growing back. She felt lighter. It was her first chance to practise what her response would be. 'Don't even ask,' she said with a smile. This was how she would handle future queries; she never wanted to use her story to garner sympathy. She would talk openly about her experience when required, but she did not offer it up for conversational fodder if there was no reason to do so. There was dignity and even a touch of humour in her response that was the hallmark of how she would carry herself later in life.

* * *

The journey to Kežmarok took several days, but when she arrived, she easily remembered the route to her aunt's house. It was late at night, and the street was shrouded in darkness. Knocking on the door, she saw a figure peering through the window to check who was there. She heard an exuberant shout. 'Mira!'

It was Heshek. He was so overwhelmed and excited to see his sister so unexpectedly that he pushed his body through the window frame and jumped to the pavement below. 'My God, I was happy he didn't break hands and feet!' said Mira. He took her in his arms, a small man with a big embrace, touching her hair and face to make sure it was really her. This was not where he lived; he happened to be travelling to town for the day and was staying at his aunt's for just one night. That is how it always was in Mira's life: coincidences folding over and over each other, forming such an elaborate pattern that it was impossible to tell where they started, and if they ever finished.

* * *

It was not only those who emerged from the concentration camps who had needed to be resourceful over the past few years. Mira realised this the next day, when Aunt Roza had a question for her. 'Do you have any jewellery with you? Any fur coats?'

Bemused, Mira shook her head no. She later found out that when other prisoners had come home, they often brought with them valuables that they had taken from the empty houses after liberation: a string of pearls, crystalware, a trinket. It had never occurred to Mira to do such a thing, but her aunt had also needed to hone her survival instinct during the preceding years.

Towards the end of the war, Roza, her husband Gerson and their young son Kurt had been hiding with Heshek and Shani; Roza and Gerson's two eldest sons, Max and Oskar, aged eighteen and twenty-three, had previously been taken to Auschwitz and killed. Max had been brilliant and handsome;

his brother Oskar a violin virtuoso, whose music teacher declared he had no further knowledge to teach him.

The Storches who survived had a remarkable tale. After the war began, Gerson had continued his work as a ladies' tailor in Kežmarok. A member of the Hlinka Guard arrived to live in town, and rented a room at the home of Gerson's friend. When this member – who called himself Mr Gula – asked his landlord to direct him to a tailor, Gerson's name came up. Gerson stitched a coat for him, and found Gula to be very civil, despite knowing Gerson was Jewish.

Not long after this, Gula became ill, lapsing into a delirium. When he was rolling around in his bed one night with a high fever, his landlord heard something startling: Gula began to recite a Jewish prayer. In this way, the man's true identity was revealed: he was Jewish himself, and had been helping Jews to hide. He had suffered a great tragedy – his wife and small daughter had been killed by the SS – and he had committed his life to saving others. When conditions in their town worsened dramatically, Gula arranged for the Storch family – along with Heshek and Shani – to leave. Shani was disguised as a member of the Gestapo, wearing a long leather coat, while Gerson carried an axe to look like a local farmer. A horse and wagon took them part of the way, and they walked for the remainder, until they came to a shepherd's hut deep in the woods: their hiding spot for the next six months. After the war, Gula moved to Israel, and was honoured for his war efforts. There, he reverted to his real name, Eliyahu Laufer. Many years later, Kurt would be reunited with him, and remembered how Laufer handed his son Danny a silver *siddur*.

* * *

When Heshek left his aunt's, he took Mira with him. For the first time in so long, she was again under her family's care. Since the end of the war, Heshek had shared a home with his brother Shani in Košice, together with a third housemate: Martin Korn, the young man who had once worked with Mira in Mr Winter's store while she was living away from home under false papers.

Some people say the world is small. Mira would have described it this way, because for her the world had infinite connections.

Martin, who now lived with her brothers, and had always been so kind to her, had a sister, Libush. She was the Jewish prisoner who had befriended the Yugoslavian women of Neustadt-Glewe, and whose group Mira had followed with their horse and cart. Far from blaming Libush, Mira understood it was a time of life and death; it brought different attributes to the fore. In Libush's case, that was perhaps an ability to fit in. 'She was not a very strong girl to stand up to anyone.' But Libush had also set into motion a series of events that ultimately saved Mira. 'I felt glad that, through her, I followed them out of Neustadt-Glewe. If not for that, where would I be?'

Mira's friends Blanka and Edit, each so pivotal during her time at Auschwitz, survived the war too. After a death march to Mauthausen concentration camp, Edit was liberated in May 1945. All of her immediate family had been killed, but she would marry and – despite being told she was sterile, having been the subject of medical experiments in camp – give birth to two daughters. She eventually moved to Sydney, Australia, and passed away in 2023.

Elza, who took on Mira's work in Auschwitz, made it through and moved to South America. Mira was never able to find her after the war. Julius Scholcz, the Blumenstocks' *arizátor*, stayed forever connected with Mira. Long after Mr Scholcz died – at the age of fifty-three, surviving his son Julla, who was killed in a motorcycle accident at twenty-one – his daughter Hilda, Mira's childhood friend, tended Dolfie's grave. Dolfie's body had been found by neighbours, who then buried him in the nearby Jewish cemetery. Hilda always cleaned his gravestone impeccably, making sure the foliage around did not grow over it. When she died in 2016, her son Ladislav did the same, continuing the role to this day.

And another connection, with a coincidence: many years ago, my sister Jeannette, a prominent psychologist, was at a conference in Canada. At the venue, she stepped into an elevator and found herself standing next to an older man who was wearing one of the conference's badges on his lapel. They made small talk, and she discovered that he hailed from Czechoslovakia. 'My mother also comes from Czechoslovakia,' said Jeannette, 'but she was born in a small town, you probably have never heard of it: Spišská Stará Ves.'

The man looked startled. 'What was your mother's original name?'

'Mira Blumenstock.'

'I am from Spišská Stará Ves too,' he said, 'and I have known your mother all my life.'

That gentleman insisted that Jeannette join him for dinner the next night, saying that another of the townsfolk, who now lived in Canada, would be there too. The man in the elevator? He was Otto Küchel, son of the respected village doctor Alexander. The other dinner guest was Bela Árje, who had also lived in her town. Both families had been among those final eight that were still left in Spišská Stará Ves when the Blumenstocks were captured. Otto was saved when the SS came to his door, and he hid on the family's balcony. He and his father's younger brother, Mikulas, a paediatrician, escaped together, taking cover in the woods. Bela had heard the sudden gunshot blast that killed Dolfie, and also had time to hide.

One of the men told Jeannette how famously beautiful Mira had been, saying, 'Your mother was the only girl who I had wanted to marry before I met my wife.'

* * *

Once she began living with her brothers and Martin, Mira set about becoming the woman of the house. She was eighteen, and had never learned how to cook properly; despite having helped her mother at home, she only knew bits and pieces, not entire recipes. Still, one night she told the men that she would be preparing a sorrel soup for them, remembering that she had always relished its tangy flavour. But she did not realise that she had to cut the stems off carefully, and so when she served the soup, it had big, hairy strings floating in it.

Recounting this story to me as she was ailing, Mira clapped her hands together and laughed with delight. I was unable to reconcile this comedic scene of domesticity with everything that had come before it.

'But it was just after the war. Weren't you traumatised? How did you go on? Didn't you feel devastated, and didn't that make it hard to live a normal life?' I asked these questions in such a rush, each one spilling over the top of the next.

My mother's response was simple. 'Ah,' she said. 'Somehow, I knew: that happened, and I've got to live with it. I was not traumatised. I was happy that I still had a family.'

* * *

Mira went back to her old house in Spišská Stará Ves only once. She knew that her father had stashed money away in three hiding spots there, so she and Heshek decided to try to retrieve it. When they arrived, they managed to find some valuables in only one of the sites, but Mira could not bear to be there for long. 'To go into the house, I had to go through the spot where my father was killed, and when I passed there, I saw him there lying in a pool of blood.' It was the one time she could not manage to subdue the memories of her past. 'I did not want to stay there for one minute,' she said. 'I was too upset. I wanted to run away very quickly.' Mira felt no sentimental attachment to this place either. 'I would never want to stay there. Never.' In 1992, she made a brief trip with her brothers to visit her father's grave once more, long after her old house had been pulled down. The cemetery was in disarray: 'A heap of gravel, everything turned over.' Still, Dolfie's tombstone was intact and well-maintained, having been tended to carefully by Hilda. On various commemorative dates, Hilda would prop a candle on its base. She always lit it for All Saints' Day.

* * *

Before long, Mira and her brothers had moved into a smaller apartment, just the three of them. Every Friday night, she would prepare a traditional Sabbath table: covering the table with a white cloth and setting it with two challah loaves, sweet wine and salt. She would light the two candles in the centre, waving her hands over the flames three times, covering her eyes to say the customary prayer. The Jewish law of lighting Sabbath candles once held a practical application, but it is also a symbol of peace, warmth and one's inner and spiritual light.

For Mira, who continued this tradition as soon as she was established in her brothers' house, it was symbolic of much more. It meant that not everything which was precious to her and her ancestors could be extinguished. 'I remember that living next to my brothers, there were other Jewish people. They said, "What's happening? How come you are [lighting Shabbat candles]?"' They couldn't understand those who retained their faith when such terrible things had happened to them. But Mira was steadfast. 'I said, "What do you mean, *How come?*" My mother did it; their parents did it. We saw it at home and that's what we are going to do. And I always did it.'

* * *

Despite her brothers welcoming her into their home, Mira knew they had their lives to live, and she was apprehensive about being a burden. Most of the people she knew were keen to get married and start families of their own. She wanted to do the same: it was the only way she could imagine accessing the kind of normal life she had experienced before the war. She wanted to belong to someone, to be part of a bigger family once more. Occasionally, she would meet a man, but sometimes her brothers did not like him, and sometimes she would break things off herself.

Again, coincidence would play a part in determining her future. She went on a holiday to the Tatra Mountains, along with her Aunt Roza. There, she met a man named Pavel, who all the single women were crazy about: he was very good-looking, worldly and well-established. Since he did not drive, he had come with his chauffeur to the Tatras. When it was time to leave, he asked Roza how she and Mira were getting home. They would take a train, Roza said. But he insisted otherwise. 'No, no, no. I would love to take you both.'

On the ride back, he invited Mira and her aunt for dinner at a fashionable restaurant. It was a lively spot: music played, and the dance floor was filled with couples. Every now and then, dinner would be interrupted by men approaching the table, asking Mira to dance. Pavel sat there watching her; he did not know how to dance well, and did not feel confident doing so.

Back in Košice, he approached Mira's brothers. He told them that his intentions were serious. 'I think your sister is very beautiful, and a nice girl, and I will look after her well,' he told them.

Heshek and Shani were not convinced, and they told Mira so. It wasn't personal; Heshek liked Pavel and considered him a friend: the two of them had worked closely together during the war, when Pavel helped forge certificates for Jews rescued from the ghettos. 'There will be plenty of boys who want to marry you,' Mira's brothers said. 'Don't rush into anything.' Pavel was thirteen years her senior, they reminded her.

But even though Mira's parents, Genya and Dolfie, had been such a love match, Mira had something else at the forefront of her mind. 'When I came out from the camp, I wanted to have more security than love,' she said. 'Everybody wanted to have somebody. He was very nice, and because he was older, I felt I would have somebody to look after me … In my mind, I always said, *It's better to be loved by someone than to love.*' She admired this man, and saw how kind and handsome he was. Even his shy manner appealed to her.

Plus, she had known him, or at least known of him, since she was very young. Her father had known him too, and had trusted him with his own life, and that of his family. Pavel's real name was David Milgrom – he was the prisoner who'd escaped Treblinka II, the one who first warned Dolfie about what was happening in the camps. If not for that, Dolfie might not have been so determined to avoid the transports; he might not have arranged a plan for his family to go into hiding. His encounter with David had helped Dolfie keep his family safe, and he'd managed to do so almost until the end of the war. While his efforts had not ultimately saved Genya, Olga, Yanchi or Dolfie himself, they had likely saved Mira, Heshek and Shani from being murdered as well.

After his escape from Treblinka II, David adopted the first name given in his false identity papers: Pavel. Everyone called him by this name. Mira presumed he preferred the nickname, but perhaps there was something else. Perhaps by ridding himself of his given name, he could exorcise the strangling cords of his past. At any rate, Pavel was the man she would marry. Her name would be Mira Milgrom, and maybe she too hoped a new name would signify a new life, a new beginning: the Mira Blumenstock who had witnessed murder and bloodshed and death could be put behind her. When Mira married Pavel, in a simple wedding in Prague on 14 July 1946, she was still only a teenager: nineteen years old.

Part Three

Twenty-nine

Not many people get to sit down with their parents and ask them things that really matter. They might inquire about the details of their day, or have them relate an anecdote from the past. But they don't focus on what really counts: the thoughts and desires and fears and longing that make a person who they are.

Interviewing my mother, I tried to ask her questions both weighty and trivial. When it came to anything biographical, I soon realised I did not know the intricacies of her life as well as I once thought. I got facts wrong, or didn't have enough of them. I had no context for the fragments I already knew. I also tried to ask her more esoteric questions. 'What was your main priority in life?' 'What has been your proudest achievement?' Sometimes, I asked her the mundane: 'What was your favourite meal growing up?' Through being a journalist, I have learned that sometimes the specific questions don't matter nearly as much as just getting the subject to talk. A pithy quote can only get you so far; it certainly counts. But it will never serve to uncover the real truth of a person.

As we got further into the process, I realised how unusual our exchange was. By asking her these questions – and really listening to her answers – I was showing her that I required a deeper knowledge of her. I was demonstrating a different kind of love: one that comes from seeking to truly understand somebody.

And more than that: talking with Mira this way gave me one last opportunity for intimacy with her that I had never imagined was still available, not at this late stage. Through the veil of her sickness, past the nausea and her swollen belly and her achiness, we were sharing moments of such beauty, I would feel dazzled by them afterwards. It was as if we had somehow managed to sneak off and have a mother–daughter holiday, one where we had spent the days laughing and crying and, most of all, loving each other fiercely.

* * *

I think about what Mira must have been like following the war. Having missed out on such a formative part of her youth, she was determined to make up for lost time. She was gay and smiling and fun, longing to partake in the world in ways that might have appeared frivolous: she liked parties and entertainment and socialising. Pavel was quite different from her; he was steady, but also serious. He had been a carer for his siblings from a young age, and he was a man who took on responsibilities with the consideration they deserved.

After seeking permission from Shani and Heshek to marry their sister Mira, Pavel explained that his savings would enable him to pay for their wedding and her bridal gown. He did not want the brothers to incur any debt; he could provide for Mira himself. The couple had an idyllic honeymoon in Italy, but by the time they returned to Prague, Mira could sense something wasn't right.

There was a 'terrible' incident over chewing gum: Mira liked having gum in her mouth, while Pavel loathed the habit. She told him she had given it up, but she continued to indulge in secret. When he walked in to find her chewing gum one day, he felt that it indicated something amiss between them, that Mira did what she wanted even knowing that it bothered her husband. He said angrily: 'I don't think we are suited.' This pronouncement upset Mira immensely, and her distress was compounded when he added, 'We can each find someone else who is better for us.' They had just come back from their honeymoon, and it was only two months since their wedding.

But soon it became clear that there was no decision to be made. Mira did not have regular periods, and a week after that argument discovered she had fallen pregnant on her wedding night. 'I was surprised, because I never counted on it, that it could happen so quickly. And that changed everything.' She was pleased, though: part of the deal she made with herself was that, having lost so many members of her family, she could build one of her own. What she might not have thought about was the fact that she was a child having a child. She felt like she had aged during the war, but other people only saw her as a teenager. When she holidayed in Switzerland, the shopkeepers always called her fräulein, the honorific for an unmarried girl. They did so even when she was heavily pregnant; she looked so very young.

In the end, her pregnancy was an easy one. Mira's life was comfortable; pampered, even. The couple settled into a routine that suited them both, moving to an apartment and hiring a woman to do much of the housework and cooking. Their son Alfred was born in 1947, less than a week before the two-year anniversary of Mira's liberation.

* * *

How had twenty-year-old Mira looked after a newborn when, by her own account, 'I never even had a baby in my hands until then'? He was born very small and blue-skinned with hair all over his face. In the delivery room, when the nurse told Pavel he had a son, he cried, '*Oy vey, gevalt!*' upon seeing him, a Yiddish exclamation of: 'Oh no!' He and his wife laughed about it afterwards.

There was no one to guide her when she hit a roadblock, when the new role of motherhood was both confusing and demanding. Mira had been nursing Fred for several weeks when her breast milk suddenly dried up over a weekend. With nowhere to turn and the shops all closed, she borrowed formula from her neighbour, not realising that it was made for a toddler, not a tiny baby. Predictably, Fred was sick with terrible diarrhoea. She later said, 'Poor Freddy, how did he survive my handling of him?' as a kind of humorous punchline. But she was also conveying how out of her depth she was, without a mother to look over her shoulder, offering advice drawn from her own experience.

By the time Fred was one year old, the couple had decided they no longer wanted to live in a Communist country, and Pavel managed to get them out of Prague under false identities in March 1948. They moved first to Belgium, where Pavel's connections secured their passports, almost impossible to obtain at the time. After spending extended periods in both Antwerp, Belgium, and Milan, Italy – more than two years all up – they decided they would make another city their permanent home. They briefly considered the newly established State of Israel, where Mira's brothers now lived, but when they visited Jerusalem, Mira was horrified: walking around she saw barbed wire, and a soldier in a tower with a machine gun. 'I started to have jitters and I felt unsafe. I couldn't take it. I said, "I cannot live in a country where I will feel like I am in a camp."'

Instead, they settled on Paris, a city that had recently been under Nazi rule but had since emerged in a kaleidoscope of brilliant lights. It was the city where Josephine Baker danced at the Folies Bergère, where composer George Gershwin found inspiration in the sound of its taxicabs for *An American in Paris*, and it was filled with the high kicks of the Moulin Rouge and the smell of Gauloises cigarettes and the pulse of vivacity and romance and colour.

It suited Mira well.

Thirty

Is it possible to make up for lost time? It is hard to know if Mira wanted to compensate for the years she had missed, or what compensation she felt she deserved. Many of her friends who had survived the Holocaust received monetary reparations from Germany after the war, but Pavel – and later my father – were opposed to her doing the same, with Manny calling it 'blood money'. Long after her death, however, I discovered she had made a claim, and had received a lump sum in 1961 of 6450 Deutsche Marks. She never got an ongoing pension, like others she knew; according to records, she had not supplied adequate documentation. I know that she would have needed the money in 1961, but perhaps she did not want any more afterwards. I wonder if she ultimately felt conflicted, as if the Nazis' crimes were being whitewashed in some way. If Germany thought, like Lady Macbeth, that it could scrub the blood from its hands, she might have been better off without it.

But when it came to living in Paris, Mira was aware of what she had missed out on in the preceding decade, and she grasped all that the city had to offer with a firm grip. From the beginning, she loved the richness of the architecture, noticing the ornamental details in residential streets: the ornate wrought-iron balconies and the elaborate door knockers; those lion heads holding brass rings in their mouths. Equally alluring were the exquisite fashions she spied in shop windows and the perfectly manicured gardens dotted throughout the city, their lawns impeccably green, the flowers as conforming as musicians in an orchestra, never deviating from their role.

What Mira liked best of all, though, was the glittering, social aspect of Paris. 'It was a very cosmopolitan way of living,' she said. 'I would sit at the rue de la Paix, at a cafe on the corner, not far from the opera house, where everyone sits on the chairs and kisses those who passed – "Hello, how are you?" It was always lively.' It is easy to imagine her sipping an espresso – she always took her coffee black, sucking it through a single sugar cube – on the streets of the Right Bank, before meandering past the enticing window display at Paquin, a famous couturier, or pausing at the entrance of family-run perfumery Rigaud, to inhale the heady scents coming from within. She also luxuriated in the long evenings. In Paris, people would not think of venturing out for dinner before 9 p.m. The grand boulevards, lit up with lamps, were always reliably vibrant, even at that late hour, when darkness shrouded the rest of the city.

As soon as she arrived in France, Mira enrolled in a language school so that she would be able to converse fluently, and she mastered French quickly. She had such a good ear for pronunciation that it was difficult to pick her as a foreigner. Life had become enchanting: she settled with Pavel and Fred in Neuilly-sur-Seine, at the western edge of Paris. While the old-style apartment overlooking a courtyard was neither large nor flashy, it was located in one of the city's most desirable suburbs: author Anaïs Nin, singer Édith Piaf and L'Oréal heiress Liliane Bettencourt all lived in Neuilly-sur-Seine at one time.

In Paris, by 1950, it was easy for women to be swept up in the city's beauty, culture and fashion. After years of deprivation, they were presented with a new kind of sensual dress – Christian Dior launched his line, which was dubbed 'the New Look', in 1947 – and stores were filled with tempting offerings such as silk and crocodile shoes, or gloves embroidered with delicate flowers. Romantic colours including pink and mauve appeared on the street, while fabrics were impossibly luxurious. Waists were nipped in, and the female form celebrated. Although none of this might have been rebellious, it was certainly revolutionary. And it appealed greatly to someone like Mira – young and pretty and slim, and with an innate appreciation for beauty.

She remembered one piece of wisdom from her grandmother Chava, and she held to it steadfastly. 'Never buy cheap clothes. They do not last, and you will always look cheap. Instead of two dresses that are cheap, buy one dress that is expensive. You will always look good and it will last twice as long.' This was what she thought about when she walked down the wide streets, heading towards the most exclusive part of the city.

'I used to go to one of the haute couture stores, and I had an arrangement with the people working there that when the season was over, about four months after, that item would be mine. I had the same figure as the models, and I would get the clothes I chose for half price. It was not Balmain, or Dior, but it was a good [label] and beautifully made, and I was very happy with everything I chose.' Souvenirs of this time would remain in her wardrobe decades later, as she could not bear to part with some of the pieces: a floral green tea dress whose flowers were embroidered with gold thread, or a metallic jacquard jacket, trimmed with beige fur. Everything was exquisitely crafted, the seams impeccable. Perhaps something else was appealing to her: if the armour she wore was undoubtedly lovely, it would be impossible to imagine the ugly scars of memory that lay underneath.

* * *

A full-time maid helped with child-minding and cleaning – allowing Mira to rise late most mornings – and cooked much of the traditional Shabbat dinner for Friday nights, since Mira still was not very adept in the kitchen. Mira had a clique of Jewish friends who were invited on Saturday evenings for a game of cards, supper and conversation. It would always remind her of days gone by in Czechoslovakia.

She and Pavel had the same aim: to look after their children and raise them well. In many ways, Pavel was a modern father, devoted to his children. Two daughters had come after Fred: Jeannette in 1951, and Lilianne in 1954. Shortly after Jeannette was born, she developed a blood disease and became ill. Pavel took it upon himself to feed her medicine throughout the nights.

When the maid had her Saturday afternoon off, he would take his young children to the nearby Jardin d'Acclimatation, an amusement park with many wildly exciting attractions, including a miniature train and an entertainment program. They would laugh at the puppet show performance, or run in the gardens. Lilianne would feed the pigeons with her father. Mira, meanwhile, would spend her afternoon at the theatre, movies or listening to talks. She particularly liked it when theatrical productions or lectures made reference to the politics of the day; she appreciated the lively debates.

The Milgroms travelled several times a year, skiing in Gstaad, Switzerland, and 'going to the most exclusive places, where I was always dressed like a queen,' said Mira. Jeannette would thrill at her mother's outfits: chic, slim-fitting dresses with high heels.

In the midst of that headiness, the children had a regimented upbringing. Pavel expected them to fall into line, to be disciplined and well behaved, and could respond harshly if they were not. Jeannette remembered feeling rather abandoned when her parents went skiing at a luxurious resort, leaving their children at an alternative ski school with the instruction that they were not to make a fuss. But there was humour in their family as well; Fred recalled a time when he was five years old, and allowed to stay up late while his parents hosted a dinner party. He begged to have some wine like the adults. A friend of his father said, 'No problem – here is some wine,' and promptly poured a drop of red into his glass of milk. The milk instantly curdled, and Fred was disgusted, while everyone around him laughed. And there were also times when their parents deviated from their strictness; Lilianne would remember Pavel leaving a tiny chocolate on top of her pillow every night.

When I asked Mira whether her marriage changed after having children, she answered, 'Put it this way: it was not a marriage where we had too much in common, if I think about it.' The two coexisted well enough, but it was clear that they were entirely different beings. Mira often looked and acted like a teenager, and had a lightness and joyfulness about her. Pavel was – and seemed – far older; his demeanour often sombre, and possessing an air of being encumbered by responsibility. Mira soon assimilated into Parisian life, adopting French idioms as if she had been born speaking them. Pavel, on the other hand, struggled to learn the language, opting instead to speak in Polish, German or Yiddish. He was altogether less talkative than she, seeming more of an observer than a participant.

They had reacted to their war experiences in opposite ways. From time to time, Mira would relate stories about her past to her children, avoiding graphic details but offering up a sense of her plight. Pavel, by contrast, who had lost his parents long ago, as well as his six siblings, never spoke about the war, about Treblinka. But his family had no doubt it had taken a toll, noting that he always needed sleeping tablets at night. As his son, Fred, remembered, 'He wouldn't talk about it, and wouldn't agree to participate when people asked if they could write about him. He didn't want to tell us kids what had happened. It was so horrific that he did not want us to dwell on the details, or romanticise them in any way – he just wanted us to move past it.'

Thirty-one

In 1959, Australia must have seemed a strange, faraway island. But Paris had lost some of its lustre for the Milgroms: Pavel was earning less than he had been before, and France's military maintained a draft system. The Korean War had unsettled Mira, and the possibility of warfare – and what that would mean for their son, if he was drafted – was at the top of Mira's and Pavel's minds.

Their close friends the Rotsteins had already emigrated to Melbourne and painted a picture of opportunity and vast expanses of land. They explained that in Australia, men were not called up to the army when they turned eighteen. That was the clincher for Mira. 'I said, "That's just [the place] for me. I have one son only, and I don't want to risk him going to war." I had seen enough of the war. I wanted to go to a country that [had] no soldiers and no war.'

Australia seemed remote, and therefore safe. Although its Jewish community was relatively small, Australia boasted the largest community of Holocaust survivors in the world, per capita, outside of Israel. By 1960, Holocaust survivors and their families would make up sixty per cent of Melbourne's Jewry.

The couple and their three children sailed to Melbourne on the SS *Oronsay* – a voyage that took four weeks – in March 1959. Fred was almost twelve; he would do his bar mitzvah in Melbourne. Jeannette and Lilianne were seven and a half and five. Pavel was horribly sick at sea, retching and groaning for days on end. Mira, though, travelled well, and she would look out over the water and wonder with excitement what lay ahead. Perhaps going through the war during her formative years meant that she was not tethered to place or even people. Australia was far from where her brothers lived – Heshek was still in Israel, in Tel Aviv, while Shani had moved to Queens, New York – but that did not seem to be a factor. Looking ahead was how she had always survived, and she would do that once more. She was no longer the girlish woman who giggled often and relished her freedom. The responsibility of three children had changed her, but her outlook had matured as well. She had been pivotal in the couple's decision to move to Australia. She was taking the reins of her life more than ever.

* * *

Melbourne was nothing like Mira had imagined: she had expected dirt roads, an open rural landscape and kangaroos bounding around. Instead, she found a city centre with large department stores and bustling streets, and green-and-yellow trams taking people from one end of town to another. It was considered something of an international city, since

Melbourne had been the first in the Southern Hemisphere to host an Olympic Games, in 1956. But the suburbs – where the family settled – were sleepier. While it was different from the country she had invented in her mind, Mira was content from the start. 'I felt right away that Australia was a quiet country, and I could make a living here. I could see it would give our family every chance to succeed. The moment I came, I loved Australia with a passion.' Even the produce tasted better: the lettuce so crisp, the tomatoes so sweet.

The Rotsteins had found the family of five some temporary accommodation: a two-bedroom flat on a busy main road, where one child had to sleep in the living room. They were not there for long, soon relocating to a small house in Hotham Street, St Kilda East. Mira remembered the passionfruit vine outside; it was a fruit she had never seen before, and a perfect symbol of the exotic new life that was now hers.

* * *

It was not easy. The children spoke no English when they arrived, although Fred, an inveterate bookworm, started reading the dictionary so he could teach himself the words. Mira again enrolled into a language school at night, and it was not long before she could speak well, although she still recalled one mishap. She met a man who had his arm in a sling, and he explained that he had broken it. 'That's terrific,' she said. He started laughing and explained that the word she wanted was 'terrible'.

Before long, the children settled into school; the girls attended the Jewish youth group Bnei Akiva on Saturdays. At a party, Pavel and Mira met a man who owned a shirt factory and had decided to liquidate it. It sounded like a good business to Pavel, who offered to buy it from him. It was in the heart of Melbourne's central business district, on Little Lonsdale Street; soon, the Milgroms took on another partner and called it Newmill. Mira worked in the factory too, and proved to be very useful: Pavel had not been able to pick up English, and so she was the one who could speak to the workers in both English and their native Italian. She also knew about fabric and textiles from her parents' store. And she provided another essential service: in-house counsellor. The workers would often argue with each other, and come to Mira with their gripes. She was only thirty-three, but they would say to her, '*Sei come una madre, aggiusti tutto!*' You are like a mother, you fix everything! It was true: through her work, she learned how capable she was in practical matters, how well she was able to navigate her way in the world.

A year had passed since they first arrived, and the family now owned a spacious house in Orrong Road. Life was different from how it had been in Paris; there was little domestic help, and everyone contributed. Jeannette loved it; she had her own bedroom, with vibrant orange curtains that she pretended were the sun visiting her. She thought they were the prettiest things she had ever seen.

But amid it all, there was a rising tension between Pavel and Mira. They did not argue, but they were not warm to one another. When the family went to the circus together, there was an unspoken agreement that the children would sit between their parents, acting as a barrier between them.

* * *

A couple of years ticked by. Mira had quickly adapted to Melbourne. She found life in her new city pleasant, and she also felt drawn to the country itself: its summery skies, its warmer winters, the easygoing banter between neighbours. There was something old-fashioned about it: milk was delivered via a horse and cart that clip-clopped up the residential streets, and shops were closed for half of Saturday and all of Sunday. There were no pavement cafes in the area, and limited alcohol was served in restaurants. At night, the streets went dark, illuminated only by occasional streetlamps, and became weighted down in complete silence, save for the chirping of cicadas if it was warm. You could count thousands of stars in the night sky. It was certainly not Paris, where you could step out of your house at midnight and still find people out and about, where there were always signs of life no matter the hour.

Mira said that Pavel never adjusted. 'He hated every minute of it, of Australia. He said that Melbourne is a cemetery – all the houses are tombstones. There are no people going around. And compared to Paris, it was a big change. He wanted very, very much to go back to Europe. And eventually he said, "That's enough. I don't want to stay in Australia anymore."' They were at an impasse; Mira felt firmly planted in her adopted city.

* * *

I had never posed these kinds of direct questions to my mother, and I suspected my siblings had not either. But decades had passed since then. 'Were you upset that your marriage was going to end?' I asked. Given the times, it was hard to believe she forged ahead without hesitation. Divorce was still highly stigmatised in the early 1960s, and Mira was living in a country far from any other family or wider support. Her response was, 'We never were very close. It was not a good marriage. We came from such different backgrounds; we could not even communicate properly, because he mainly spoke Yiddish, and I learned my Yiddish from him.' She added that there was no communication in a wider sense: 'Whatever I wanted to do, I could not share with him. And in a way, nor could he with me. After fifteen years, we had lived that way long enough.' She was not the sort of person who would hold on to a disintegrating marriage for the status it offered, or for the illusion it presented to the world. If you were someone who had once lost everything? Ending a marriage was easier, I suppose.

Pavel made the painful decision to leave. He acted decently, and there was no acrimony between them. 'Pavel was a very considerate person,' Mira said. 'He was always fair. I cannot say one bad thing about him. It was just that – he agreed that we were not made to be together.'

Pavel hated the thought of his children living in a different country from him, but both he and Mira lacked an understanding of the ways in which divorce might affect everyone. For them, the decision was straightforward: it would be easier if Pavel left, since the children wouldn't have to bear the shame of a broken family. There was some discussion about him taking the children to live in Israel, but it was decided that they were better off in Australia with their mother. For Pavel, it was a sacrifice he was willing to make for the good of his family. But neither of them had the emotional foresight to execute this well: there was no conversation to prepare their children or let them know what was happening. Jeannette only realised her father was leaving when he had his suitcase already in hand; in a panic, she rushed to her bedroom to grab something she could give him, choosing a basket she had made in a craft class. Upon arrival, he sent her a photo of himself cradling it in his arms.

Before Pavel left, he purchased a crumbling but stately Victorian mansion, subdivided into apartments, that had been passed in at auction. He saw that it could be both a home for his family and provide income for their future. Afterwards, letters addressed to the children would show up at their house frequently, written in Yiddish. Mira would translate, since they increasingly could not remember what the words meant. Every year, one of the children went overseas to visit him; it was too expensive for them all to go together. Mira never spoke ill of Pavel, and when packages bearing gifts arrived for them, she would say, 'Look at what your father sent! How wonderful is he?'

Pavel moved to Belgium, and lived there until his death in April 1984, never remarrying. After he died, Lilianne flew to his home to take care of his estate, packing up his belongings and closing his accounts. She stumbled upon something heartbreaking: an old letter from Mira, which revealed that Pavel had wanted to reunite with her after he had left. It was clear, by her words, that she had said no. And also, correspondence from another woman whom Pavel had met in Belgium. Lilianne managed to track her down, and learned something startling: 'I loved Pavel,' the woman said, 'but he never stopped being in love with Mira.'

Thirty-two

Mira found someone to take over Pavel's share of Newmill: a man who was part of her circle of Czechoslovakian émigrés in Melbourne. Menachem – Manny – Unreich had come to Australia a decade before her, in 1949. Born into a very religious family in Bratislava in 1916, he had fled Czechoslovakia early, heading by boat to Palestine when he was just nineteen. Eventually landing in Paris, he enlisted in the Czechoslovak Army in 1939, serving until 1946. After fighting in Dunkirk on D–Day, he was awarded a medal of bravery from Czechoslovak president Edvard Beneš.

Manny's life had been colourful, but also marred by tragedy: the same month that Mira, Genya and Yanchi were sent to Plaszow, Manny's parents Shalom and Rachel had been crammed into cattle trucks that were headed for Auschwitz. They had also been in hiding, but emerged when they heard a rumour that there would be an amnesty for Jews on Yom Kippur, the Day of Atonement. They were captured on 28 September 1944, together with their daughter Reitzi, her husband Lazar and their grandchildren Judith, eight, and Miriam, six. Several days later, on 5 October, all six of them were murdered.

But Manny had also lived voraciously – residing in London, Paris and Palestine, and once briefly working for Golda Meir as a bodyguard and informal translator before she was elected prime minister of Israel. He had been an amateur wrestler in his youth, and was built like each of his six brothers: broad-shouldered and solid. He had a thick head of black hair, full lips and plenty of self-confidence. When Mira met him, he was a bachelor in his mid-forties with no shortage of female admirers, many of whom compared him to Clark Gable. He was eleven years older than Mira, and she soon found that she looked forward to seeing him at work.

'He was a very handsome man, but at the time I was not interested in other people,' she said. 'I had my problems; I had my children to look after. But when he became a partner in the factory, of course I saw him every day. He was very courteous, perfect in English, fluent in French. And he was very good at his job, because he was a wonderful salesman. He did not have much knowledge about garments, but he very quickly stepped in. And with him, we started getting bigger orders; he knew how to persuade people.'

Gradually, she began inviting him to Friday night dinners, and he loved the atmosphere she created. He was charmed by her children, and as a bachelor who lived alone, he adored her cooking and the way in which she kept her home so beautifully. Not too long after they began working together, they fell in love.

* * *

Manny was not the only one who commanded the attention of others. When he invited Mira to be his guest at a large function – held by a Jewish organisation in an old hotel in Elwood which housed an impressive ballroom – she knew exactly what to wear. She selected a black dress made from moiré, a silky matte fabric that creates the illusion of flowing water with its rippling appearance. It had a tight bodice, long sleeves and three folds at the rear, finished with a giant bow that spanned almost the entire back of the gown. When she described it to me, I tried to imagine what everyone else present that night thought when they caught sight of her: a small woman with dancing eyes and engaging dimples, resplendent. When I was a child, family friends always reiterated how glorious-looking my mother had been; a show-stopper. But Mira only remembered the gown. 'Nobody could believe it, because I still had the dress from Paris, elegant and beautiful, and so everybody talked about me. Even years later they said: "We can't forget how you looked at that ball."'

* * *

In the end, she was the one who proposed. 'I said, "Look, we are close enough – do you think you want to marry?"'

Mira and Manny wed on 5 September 1965, at East Melbourne Hebrew Congregation, when she was thirty-eight and he forty-nine. They did not tell anyone they were going to do so; Mira said they announced the news to the three children only after the fact: 'We came in and I said, "You can say *mazel tov* – we got married!'" To her, this method was the smoothest way of handling it – 'We did not want to make any fuss about it' – but there was likely another reason that she did it this way. It meant there would be no room for discussion, for objection; it was a fait accompli. She was Mira Unreich now, and she gave birth to me, Rachelle, almost a year later in 1966.

I asked my mother if she was ever concerned that she would be alone after her divorce, or if she expected to meet someone again. 'I was never worried,' she said. 'I was so full of myself! I was confident.' She said it flippantly, but there was a truth within: she had grown into a woman who could hold her own, who knew what she wanted. She had no need to depend on anyone else. She had developed skills that she was proud of, and rightly so.

* * *

I remember standing up in my cot as a baby and calling to my mother downstairs. She would appear, and my refrain was always the same: 'More *amour*!' It was Mira's cue to sing me my favourite lullaby, which was never intended for babies: an Yves Montand love song, 'Amour, Mon Cher Amour'. My mother sang a much more elongated version than Monsieur Montand, her voice starting in a deep register, slowing the words down. It was so soothing to me, and I remember that I was only able to settle when I heard it repeated several times, her hand gently patting my head in unison with the song.

It was not until I had children that I realised how much she sang to me when I was young. She would make up little ditties of her own, one of which incorporated my Yiddish name and middle name, Simonne, as well as the German word for belly. Included were invented words, like the one she substituted for dimple. 'Rachelle, has got a little bachele/ Simkele, has got a little dimkele. Tra la la la, tra la la la boom boom boom!'

As a mother, Mira was different with me than she had been with her other children. I was born nineteen years after Fred and was the youngest in the family by twelve years. When Fred was young, she was young too, and was often mistaken for his sister. She had not yet worked out what she wanted or where her strengths and weaknesses lay; she had only just started to develop as an adult. But she knew she longed to experience life and not be a bystander, so while she loved her children deeply, her life did not revolve around them. They, instead, orbited her.

After Pavel left, she forged a tight-knit bond with her older children, relying on them to help her cook and keep house while she spent all day at work. She said she found working 'wonderful', because it made her feel self-sufficient, but the children kept her morale up as well.

'They were such good children. They would be at home after school, looking through the window to see when my car was coming. Then they would say, "She's here, she's here!" They would put on the kettle, make me a coffee, prepare my chair and little stool to sit on – everything for me to relax when I came home from work. And they received very little pocket money from me, but still they saved for my birthday. They bought such expensive things! Once, they bought me an evening dress with a jacket, with a fur trim around it. And another time, I said I didn't have any decent dishes, so they bought me a set. I don't even know how they managed it. They looked after me, really.'

When I was born, Mira was thirty-nine — far older than any of my contemporaries' mothers. Many of my friends gravitated to my house because she was the archetypal mama, looking almost like an illustration from a children's book. She was rounded, smiling and often wore an apron. Although she worked long hours — managing her investment property and, for a while, launching an import business — she was always there to greet me when I returned home from school. She was affectionate and vivacious, and accommodating to my needs. For example, when she said I could redecorate my bedroom, we engaged in countless discussions over the perfect shade of lilac paint for the walls.

Not that I always appreciated her efforts. I had a ferocious temper as a child, and sometimes I would yell or fling clothes across the room if I was angry. I routinely slammed doors and stomped up the stairs; I was not like her other children, who had been much more compliant. But, then, she had not really had the experience of being at home alone with a young child, having always had hired help in Paris. One can only imagine how essential their nanny Giselle had been; when Giselle became a mother herself, she felt so attached to Lilianne that she gave her own daughter the same name. Since she wasn't used to handling a newborn on her own, Mira relied on the assistance of my older siblings. Once, unable to settle me, she knocked on Jeannette's bedroom door at midnight and gave me to her to rock. On some of those restless nights, my father would put me in the car and drive for hours along the bay until I fell asleep.

My father also indulged me terribly when I was little, much to my mother's chagrin. 'Every day, when Manny came home and we sat down to eat dinner, you said, "Daddy, did you bring me something?" And he would take out a little present from his pocket, and often even two or three. I became very angry that he bought so many presents all the time; that's not good. But he could not stop. One day, he brought one present. And you said, "Is that all?" I gave him a look and said, "You see? If you don't stop, she will want to have the world." So he stopped.'

Sometimes when I was young, I butted heads with my mother, but at other times, she seemed like the person who understood me best. When I was seven and announced that I wanted to create a perfume business, she helped me set up a table on the pavement outside our house and gave me empty bottles to use. And then, when no passers-by bought my wares, she purchased three of the bottles herself, tipping the vials so that drops of the concoctions inside – which included ingredients like mouth wash and bubble bath – spilled onto her wrist. She sniffed theatrically, and said, 'Oh, how beautiful this fragrance is!'

* * *

My parents liked to entertain friends, often hosting card parties that were so overflowing with couples – sometimes sixty people came – that men and women had to be separated into two groups in order to contain the crowd. Everyone arrived dressed in impeccable outfits, even when the games took place in the daytime. One group would play on several card tables upstairs, and the remainder would have the same set-up below, with the rounds of games occurring simultaneously. Halfway through, the adults congregated in the dining room, where a bounteous spread of food awaited them, and the sounds of their bellowing laughter could be heard from every pocket of our home. My father would usually beckon me to his side for good luck, and then let me squeeze in next to him and hold his cards, laughing off the mild griping of the other card players when his fortunes suddenly improved with my presence. I remember the clickety-clack of the women's perfect red nails on the tabletops while they considered their next move, and the ashtrays soon overflowing with cigarette butts. The adults would pinch my cheek and call me 'Rachi', and sometimes I would hide underneath one of the tables while they played, hoping to pick up a piece of their exuberance and joie de vivre from the floor.

Thirty-three

All Mira's life, there were strange coincidences, incidents that made her believe in – what? Serendipity? Spirituality? These things were more than happenstance, she knew that.

When Mira was living in Prague with Pavel, they had to furnish their home from scratch. My mother had not been able to save much from her childhood; she had a few precious photos of her parents and of herself, but little else. So much of what made up a Jewish home needed to be purchased anew: candle holders for lighting candles on the Sabbath eve, a Kiddush cup to hold the sacramental wine and a set of *machzors*, the Jewish prayer books that were relevant for various holidays – including Passover, Yom Kippur and Rosh Hashana.

Pavel went to an antique store for the *machzors*, chancing upon an older, used set that looked just like something the previous generation might have used. Its age gave it an authenticity and familiarity; a nod to the family heirlooms that ought to have been theirs. This set was bound in black leather with gold monogrammed initials on each cover, and contained the Hebrew script inside, together with a German translation. After Pavel left Australia, the treasured set became Mira's own, and one that she would take to *shule* on every holy festival.

She had been married to Manny for many years when, during one of the Jewish holidays, he was ready to leave for synagogue and realised that he had misplaced his own prayer book. 'Can I borrow yours?' he asked, so Mira reached for the corresponding one in her set. When she handed it to him, he looked stunned. He turned it around and around again, examining the cover. He leafed through the pages, stopping at certain sections. And then he touched the monogram with his fingers. The initials were plain to see: *S.U.* He looked up at Mira. 'This once belonged to my father, Shalom Unreich,' he said. Neither of them could quite believe it. Long before Manny had even met Mira, his future wife was reading from his father's *machzor*, back in Prague. The set had travelled from Czechoslovakia, to Antwerp, to Milan, to Paris and finally to Melbourne, before landing in Shalom's son Manny's hands once more.

In Judaism, there is the concept of *beshert*, which means destiny. Most Jewish people use the term when describing their soulmate, lifting from the segment of the Kabbalah, the school of Jewish mysticism, and the belief that husband and wife are half-souls until they find one another. But strictly speaking, *beshert* is the suggestion of divine providence. Was it preordained that the *machzor* had travelled this route, connecting two people who had met by chance, so far from their original birthplaces? The word '*machzor*' means cycle, but the root of the word in Hebrew also means 'to return'. For me, it is hard to explain the existence of the *machzor* in any other way.

* * *

As we worked through the chronology of her life, it came time for me to ask Mira about her relationship with my late father, Manny, who had died in 2005. It's tricky stuff; does anyone want to speak to their parents about that? From my point of view, my father had been loving and warm, and tried his best to navigate the difficult waters of being a step-parent. Whenever he was asked how many children he had, he would always say four, never employing the accepted terminology of blended families, such as 'half-sister' or 'stepchild'. He worked hard to support us and upheld values of humility and modesty. One of the worst insults he would use was to say someone was 'showy'. He always tried to be charitable, but wanted no recognition; he would rather do a good deed anonymously than put his name to it.

He had gorgeously curvy handwriting – at seventeen, he had studied calligraphy in Vienna – and loved all animals, but particularly dogs and horses. He made magic happen in my childhood: there was often a horse at my birthday parties, and once he phoned the Bacchus Marsh Lion Park to see if he could rent a lion cub for the day. Wisely, they refused. He was generous and giving, and a willing raconteur: he always had a story at the ready, although sometimes you had to buckle up for a good long while. He died two months shy of his ninetieth birthday, when a combined heart attack and stroke caused his organs to shut down. We had a few days to say goodbye to him, but it was not a gentle farewell, fraught with the confusion and terror brought by hospitals and sudden decision-making.

In my head, I had a firm view of what my parents' marriage had been like, but if asked to describe it, I would have chosen my words carefully. As my father got older, he became difficult and demanding. And even when I was younger, I remembered his bursts of temper. He would get red-faced and shout loudly, and while those episodes passed quickly, I couldn't always wipe off the drops of those thunderstorms so speedily. I braced myself to talk to my mother about him, not sure what I would learn.

'Did you feel like you were in love?' I asked. I can see now that there was trepidation in that question, but Mira was clear. 'I was very much in love with Daddy. It was very beautiful. He used to leave little cards with messages on the car window; he always did something that made me feel like I counted so much in his life. He was a very beautiful lover, very much so. I was very lucky to have found someone like that, who had no attachments and accepted a woman with three children. And he was very good to the children, too.'

I had never heard my mother speak quite so explicitly about her marriage before. It was a turning point for me, making me realise that while a child may have their own perspective on a relationship, it is the person involved whose opinion matters most, and who is likely more accurate as well. Their arguments had left such an impression on me that I let them colour my entire view of my parents' connection. But looking back, perhaps those moments of volatility did not happen as often as I'd thought, or did not cut as deeply as I had imagined.

'What about the fights you had?' I asked.

Mira dismissed them with a wave of her hand. 'Oh, we were passionate people.'

What I had completely discounted, I realised, were the things that made up the fabric of their daily lives. Every night after dinner they played cards together, and I would usually find them in gales of laughter, my father pretending to have been 'bamboozled' by my mother's skills. Sometimes he would throw the cards in the air in a mock tantrum, and they would be cackling together when I walked in. I had no idea that Manny also slipped love letters into Mira's lunchbox when she went to work, or that he had made her feel so special.

But I felt it, because by the time I was ten, it was just the three of us in the house. We went on holidays: driving to Phillip Island for the weekend and walking around the rocky shore. Or, in winter, we would fly to Surfers Paradise, which I remembered as a heady mix of hotel swimming pools and pink lemonade that arrived with a plastic flamingo perched on the glass. On those warm days in Queensland we would go to the beach and my father would carry me on his shoulders into the crashing waves, his arms smelling like sea salt and suntan lotion. My mother would remain on the sand, sitting on a towel; she never wanted to go more than knee-deep into the ocean. One night we hired a 'Silly Cycle', a wheeled contraption where riders could sit side by side on a bench seat, each with a set of pedals. I was wedged between my parents, waving at tourists as we passed by. In those times, I felt cocooned in love, and I always presumed it was their love for me – but maybe it was their love for one another, too.

Their friends would later describe them as social and fun-loving, and they were the type of couple who made their presence felt: my mother for her sophistication and warmth and the light she brought with her, and my father for his charisma and ability to talk to anyone – not to mention his desire to talk to everyone. He would converse with business leaders easily, but I also remember how he would take me to visit the local aged-care home when I was little. I would sit silently in a chair, bored and fidgety, while he would listen to old people chatter away, never seeming to tire of their conversation.

Interviewing my mother about these times, I realised: her answers led me to see not only my parents' lives differently, but my own as well.

Thirty-four

When I was in my early twenties, living in Los Angeles, I came across a notice about a second-generation Holocaust group that was welcoming new members. I thought it sounded interesting. In Melbourne, I did not know many people my age whose parents had lived through the Holocaust, despite the influx of Jewry to Australia after World War II. Some of my friends had grandparents who had been through the war, but not parents. In my case, since my mother had given birth to me late in life – she was close to forty, which was ancient for childbirth in the 1960s – the offspring of her contemporaries were generally a decade older than me, or more. In addition, I had not heard of many people as young as her surviving the concentration camps; children and the elderly shared the lowest rate of survival, and age was a highly influential criterion in the 'selection' process at camp.

Arriving at the meeting, I was unsurprised to discover that most members were considerably older than me. They *looked* older than me. I was twenty-three, wearing acid-wash jeans and an oversized sweater, while they were all in suits. When it was time to go around the room exchanging stories, everyone nodded their heads in recognition with whoever held the floor. I shuffled my feet and considered leaving halfway through. I could not make sense of the things being said. They all seemed to speak of parents who were too scared to let them ride bicycles, who hoarded food, who looked sad at best and panicked at worst for most of the time. These parents talked about the Holocaust constantly, or not at all, keeping their secrets in a vault while everyone around them banished decades of history from conversation. The survivors were largely traumatised, and their children carried that trauma, like runners who had been passed a baton in a relay race.

I thought about my cheerful, ever-smiling mother, who walked down Carlisle Street with purpose and vigour as she did her weekly errands. If you accompanied her, you felt like you were in the company of a celebrity, as bankers and fruiterers alike popped out of their premises to greet her by name. I thought of the woman who had raised me to be brave, who was unwaveringly supportive when I announced that I was going to UCLA in Los Angeles to study. And I remembered the first overseas trip I took with my parents, when people mistook my mother as a citizen of their own in every new country we visited. She passed as Greek in Athens; she spoke fluent Italian in Rome and exquisite French in Paris. Perhaps it was because she fit in so well, with her European sensibilities, but in each place, people gravitated towards her, charmed by her smile and laugh and manner. There was a light in my mother that so many others around her saw and that nothing had managed to dim.

* * *

I had only ever known my mother with a tattoo: that dirty blue prisoner registration number that was etched onto her forearm. A souvenir from Auschwitz: number A-26103. After the war, she said that some people would look at her tattoo and not know what it meant. 'What is that?' they would ask. And she would have to explain it to them.

An oversight: I never talked to her about it, not in detail; never questioned who did it and how. 'Did it hurt?' I vaguely remember asking her when I was younger, and she told me, 'Not really,' but I don't know how accurate that was; I imagine that what she meant was that it was less painful than so many other horrors she endured.

When I learned that Lali Sokolov was a prisoner *Tätowierer*, or tattooist, at Auschwitz, I wondered if he had performed the task; if he had been the one to pierce the outline of her serial number into her skin. Later research revealed that he had not – a work detail known as an *Arbeitskommando* was responsible for doing it when Mira was there. Still, my parents were very close to Lali and his wife Gita in Melbourne. Did Mira first meet them in Auschwitz? I never thought to ask; I did not even know which of my parents' friends had been in concentration camps and which had not, although I later found out it was most of them.

But it made sense that they gravitated towards each other. My father, also born in Czechoslovakia, had escaped the country early on, but his parents and eldest sister were killed in Auschwitz. And Mira once said a sad thing. When she was in camp, the prisoners all held tight to one belief. 'We thought that when we were going to get out of camp, we are going to tell the world [what happened]. People who will find out about what we went through will be very sympathetic to us and help us. But that was not the case, not at all. People did not really want to help the prisoners who came out.

'People asked, "How come you came back?" They thought maybe we were guilty of being not good, being a collaborator or something like that. Otherwise, how did we survive and not the others? They couldn't understand: if things were so terrible at camp, then how come we came back? Why were we not also killed?'

She said it was mainly Jewish people who thought this way. 'A lot of girls who survived, when they later went out with a boy, the boy said, "I don't think I can marry a girl who came from camp." It took a long time for people to realise that we were victims. And so that was very sad.'

As a result, she said, 'The boys and girls and families who went through camp came together. They knew that people who came back were innocent. And also, other people did not really understand what happened. If you stayed behind, if you were on Aryan papers, or converted, you lived more or less in a good way. And even straight after the war, I don't remember reading that much in the newspapers about what happened in the Holocaust. People knew, but not too much.'

Perhaps that was also why Mira would not shy away from addressing what had happened to her when asked: she could not countenance those misconceptions. She would never have dreamed of deliberately covering up her tattoo with clothing or make-up.

In 2013, my sister Lilianne, an artist, produced a collection of black-and-white photos, titled *Shadows*, which were exhibited in the US and Melbourne. In the series, Mira's numbered tattoo is projected through shadows onto Lilianne's skin – on her forearm in one, and across her chest in another. But in the photos, the number is giant-sized, spanning half her arm, from her elbow to her wrist. When I asked Lilianne why she chose that subject, she responded: 'I realised just how deeply her tattoo was tattooed into my own soul, just as it was tattooed onto her skin.' She explained how Mira's Holocaust experiences had formed part of her psyche, and while she could not grasp the horrors that our mother had gone through, some of it had managed to transfer to us all.

The generations who have come after Holocaust survivors cannot help but see these tattoos as a blight, forever marking trauma in such a visible way. But what we sometimes forget is what they signified: in Auschwitz, if you received the tattoo, it was better than the alternative. If they did not mark your skin this way, it meant that you were about to be put to death. Only those who were sent to work – who were not elderly, too young or infirm – were allowed to live, and therefore received a tattoo. Having one meant that you had a slight chance of survival, however remote that possibility.

Thirty-five

I had been raised with the idea that life did not end on earth –
that after death there was the *Olam Ha-ba*, the world to come.
In my mid-twenties, I did not think about any of this terribly
deeply, or even at all. Like most young adults, I was more
concerned with the minutiae of my day-to-day, and not the
wide-lens perspective.

My accident in Thailand in 1992 happened two weeks
after I had interviewed a psychic for a magazine article. She
did not take herself too seriously and nor did I; she was well
known in Sydney's Kings Cross for reading tarot cards, and
she told me she did it to give hope to street kids and to distract
herself from her own tendency towards addiction. Still, right
before I left her, she turned to me and said, 'Be careful of fast
drivers.'

I didn't pay much heed. She dressed in costume, wearing
a silver headscarf on her greying hair and oversized, dangly
earrings in the shape of stars. She had a crystal ball on her table
as a prop, and she confided in me that the attribute she relied

on most heavily was goodwill rather than clairvoyance. So when she said those words to me in farewell, I merely thanked her politely and hurried away.

In a fortnight's time, my mother would come to rescue me in Bangkok, and dream that her parents had intervened to save me from certain death. Instead of starting back in my magazine office job that Monday, I was in a Thai hospital. On Monday morning, a phone call came in to my Sydney desk, with the psychic on the end of the line. She was harried, fluttery. She asked my colleague Megan, who had answered the call, if there was any news of me. Megan had learned about the accident only minutes before, and said I was recuperating overseas. 'Are you sure she's alive?' asked the psychic. Assured that Megan's information was correct, she passed on a message for me: as soon as I returned to Sydney, I was to phone her.

Five months and a dozen operations later, I did. Even though she had been told I survived, she was surprised to hear my voice. 'You were meant to die in that accident, did you know that?' she said with not an ounce of self-doubt.

In bed that night, I closed my eyes and said a quiet prayer of thanks to my grandparents, just in case she was right.

* * *

Something else.

Two years after that accident, I moved to New York City, and one of my best friends there was a guy named Adam. We often did things together: I travelled with him to his birthplace of Altoona, Pennsylvania, for his family's Passover Seder, where I met his band of brothers, who were just like him: tall and dark and entertaining. While they played basketball outside I wandered through their childhood bedrooms, looking for clues about who they were and how they were raised.

Adam enjoyed being my perennial plus one, and once he accompanied me to a movie premiere. I had learned to play it cool around the famous set, pretending I didn't know who they were when we passed each other. But I kept finding Adam tucked away in corners, pulling a celebrity talk show host aside for a chat, or telling a film ingenue how pretty she looked.

'You can't do that,' I said to him disapprovingly.

'Why not?' he countered. 'Maybe they want to meet me.'

When he got sick, I sent him chicken matzo ball soup from Second Avenue Deli, and when he got much, much sicker, I visited him in hospital and held his hand.

Adam died when he was thirty-four, having recently moved to Los Angeles, where I'd paid him a brief visit. We spent the day squeezing in everything that we could think of: rollerblading along Venice Beach, eating sushi in Santa Monica, star-spotting in Hollywood. When I arrived back to Australia, he sent me an email: 'LA was brilliant in your reflection.' What I didn't say was how brilliant I felt in his.

A few months after that trip, I received a phone call from my mother, telling me to come to her house urgently. I knew something terrible had happened, but I didn't know who was involved, or what had taken place. When I arrived on her doorstep, she told me everything she knew: Adam had died, having taken his own life a few hours earlier. He had jumped off the rooftop of the building opposite his apartment. I was one of his first friends to be notified.

For a long time, I tried to make sense of it. Yes, he had been sick; he had been diagnosed with colitis, and his pain and suffering with it was intense. Yes, he was on medication that carried a risk of causing psychosis. But he had also put fresh food in his fridge the day before; he had accepted an invitation for later that week. I could not understand it, but one of his brothers told me to stop trying: 'It doesn't change what's already happened,' he said.

I was engaged to be married when Adam died; he had promised he would come to the wedding. Four months after his death, I got married underneath a *chuppah* – a canopy – made up of forty-nine pieces of fabric that various friends and family members had decorated. On one square, Adam's mother had placed a photo of her son.

When I first picked up the large piece of material – sewn together like a patchwork quilt – from the seamstress, she pointed to the photo of Adam. 'What happened to him?' she asked.

My eyes pricked with tears. 'That's my friend Adam. He died suddenly.'

'Ah,' she responded, as if that made sense to her. 'When I started sewing that piece, I saw him in this room, kneeling on the floor. He didn't say anything; he just smiled. I knew he was telling me he was okay.'

When I told her, through sobs, that he had been a very, very good friend, she said, 'I could tell he was a good person, because he had such a nice, warm smile.'

Thirty-six

After marrying at the age of thirty-three, I tried to have children for years. Despairing that I would never be able to do so, I dreamed one night that I did: a boy and a girl, both with curly hair, sitting on the front steps of Mira's house. It was summer, and they were waving to me and smiling. The dream was not significant just for that image, but also because when I saw them, I felt something shift in my heart. It felt like certainty had been poured into it. When I woke, I did not dare hope that the dream was prophetic in any way. It was merely comforting, I told myself. And it did comfort me; I held tight to that image for a while, like a photo hidden in a locket. I did not get pregnant so soon after that dream, but once my children, Julian and Zoë, had been born, I remembered it again. They didn't exactly look like those two dream children, but they shared similarities: the curly hair, the wide smiles, the boy a little older than his sister. When Zoë was a small child, she said apropos of nothing, 'Before I was born, I was waiting for you to be ready, and then I came down.'

* * *

What did I know about mothering? A lot, it turned out. Mira had taught me that babies wanted to be sung to, and there was no song that was not worth repeating at least six times. She taught me that children hate scratchy clothes but love soft blankets and warm socks. That a sore tooth could be fixed if you took a swig of Serbian plum brandy called slivovitz and held it on the achy place on your gum for five minutes. Colds could be remedied by filling a soup pot with boiling water and then resting your face over it, covering your head with a towel until the sweat from your cheeks mixed with the steam and dripped into the water below. She believed that roller skates were a fad and bicycles were an investment, and it was okay to buy your daughter a brass bed with a double mattress when she was thirteen if she promised that she would keep it forever and even take it to her matrimonial home one day. I never did take that bed to another home. It stands in my mother's house today, a reminder of how much Mira wanted to make my dreams come true.

* * *

My children adored their Nana Minnie, a name with which Mira was anointed when her eldest grandson, Adam, could not pronounce 'Mira' properly. Going to her house was a grand adventure for them, and because she threw out nothing, her cupboards contained everything. When I was growing up, there was no fancy-dress party that she could not fashion a costume for: Roaring Twenties flapper! 1970s hippie! If someone had a need for a long blonde wig and platform shoes with cork heels, she would magic them up from a box in her attic.

She threw herself into everything – she hated a job done poorly – but her enthusiasm was at its peak whenever there was a Jewish festival to celebrate. For our Passover Seders – the ritual feast that rejoices in the Jews being freed from slavery in ancient Egypt – Mira would exchange the regular dining chairs for our lounge room's wide armchairs and couches, cushioning them further with fluffy pillows and doonas. It was in line with the Haggadah's requirement that we 'recline' during the meal, but none of my Jewish friends conducted their Seders this way. Surrounded in a cloud of feather-filled bedding at the table, with the meal invariably stretching out until midnight, those two annual Seder meals would feel dreamlike.

Growing up, my childhood cubby house, situated in our front garden, would convert to a sukkah for the holiday of Sukkot, commemorating the time when Jews wandered the desert for forty years. The roof lifted up on a hinge to reveal the stars, while the top was covered with palm leaves, and my family squeezed into this little dwelling for a week's worth of meals. Inside, Mira made it look like a royal's hiding spot in a faraway land, the walls adorned with ornate rugs and coloured fairy lights strung up around the ceiling. My father Manny's creations were displayed on the walls: he folded and cut layers of coloured craft sheets to make three-dimensional works of art; delicate pieces of origami-like beauty. At the time, I barely took note of my mother's efforts; I was so accustomed to her preparing and cooking for weeks in advance of these holidays that I did not fully appreciate the energy she expended on them.

Later, Mira's grandchildren always anticipated her bustling family dinners, over-catered with food and with everything else too: noise, laughter, people. There was a happy chaos about those meals; often a dish would come out missing an ingredient, or burned around the edges. She took it in her stride, and if someone poked fun at her efforts, she laughed along with them.

* * *

'Where would you go to again, if you could travel anywhere?' I asked my mother. She had seen so much of the world, living in eight cities and five countries. She knew how to immerse herself in a place and not just observe it. When I was thirteen, she and my father took me to visit Paris. We traipsed to Notre-Dame, where we stood in front of a shrine filled with red and white candles, framed by a stained-glass window overhead. When we walked around the cathedral, Mira recounted the plot of Victor Hugo's novel *The Hunchback of Notre-Dame*, which she had once read in its original French. On that same trip, we dined with her best friend Betty, who took us down a cobblestoned street until we came to a petite bistro where we sat at the bar. There, my mother urged me to try garlic snails, dripping in butter. Although she observed kosher dietary restrictions back in Melbourne – snails were definitely not allowed – she made exceptions to those rules, and partaking in a one-off experience trumped everything else. Once, on a weekend trip to Tasmania, she shocked me by ordering bacon for breakfast. 'You should know what you're missing out on!' she declared.

She embraced the expansiveness that travel could bring; she was almost seventy when she came to stay with me in New York for a fortnight, and happily accompanied me to see a band at a dive-y, late-night bar in the West Village where the cigarette smoke was thick, the instruments were played at a deafening volume and the singer hopped onto tables and gyrated his hips for the female patrons. I remember her gaiety on that evening. I saw her willingness to see the city through my eyes.

When it came to listing places she would have liked to see one more time, Mira immediately named three. One was Saint-Paul de Vence, in the south of France, which she described as a breathtakingly picturesque village, home to the most memorable hotel she had ever stayed in: La Colombe d'Or. Its walls were decorated with a startling array of paintings by famous artists, who had once exchanged artwork for a room there or a meal at their renowned restaurant. She had seen up close the works of Marc Chagall, Joan Miró and Pablo Picasso, and she marvelled over the combination of fine art, countryside and sophistication.

Also high on the list were Zürich, in Switzerland, which she loved for its sweeping landscapes and refined people, and Venice, which magnified all the charm of Italy in a unique setting. After she died, my first overseas trip was a pilgrimage to Venice in summer, where I looked like any other tourist riding in a gondola. But as I floated under the arched bridges, I was whispering my mother's name into the canals.

Thirty-seven

Why had my mother survived the Holocaust, when so many had not? Mira attributed some of her survival to the goodness of those 'who helped me without getting benefit from it themselves. I didn't have anything to give, and they helped me.' But what was the quality inherent in her that made them want to help? 'Honesty, and not being too demanding,' she said.

I thought about what that meant, her honesty. The Yiddish word *erlekh* means honest, and it is used to describe somebody who is virtuous. The word can imply spirituality – a purity with which somebody upholds the Jewish laws. Mira had a belief in a purpose higher than herself, and it was so pure and clear that I think others could not help but be drawn to her.

* * *

On birthdays, Mira never failed to write me fulsome cards. By 2012, I had been separated for a number of years, amicably co-parenting two children with my ex-husband. Mira had approached the demise of my marriage in a practical yet foresighted way, always ensuring there was a seat at her Shabbat table for the man I had married. But even though I had been able to build a rich, supportive and rewarding friendship with him, the end of a marriage is difficult. That year, Mira began my birthday card effusively. 'My darling daughter Rachelle,' she wrote. 'What can I say, and how can I express my feelings today? First, I want to thank you for being such a lovely daughter. I know I can count on you when I need you. Your willingness and readiness are beyond belief. I do love you more than you know.' And at the end: 'I am praying to the Almighty always, to bring a lasting love in your life. I hope it will happen this year. Don't lose hope! THE HAPPINESS IS NEAR.' The last, in capital letters.

It was an odd sentiment for her to write. Growing up, she had never once told me I needed to find a husband; rather, I learned to say, 'I am going to university,' at a very young age, parroting what she continually reinforced. After my separation, Mira reassured me that I would be fine no matter what happened. I knew this would be so, since I had an example in her – someone who never complained of feeling lonely or bored, who always managed to return to her buoyant self after challenges. She had always been fine, alone or otherwise. I was sure I would be fine, too.

* * *

Mira's 'take care of yourself' attitude, drummed into her by her father, sometimes meant that she refused to ask for help at all. When she was well into her eighties, she fell down in a car park after buying fruit. She shooed away the passers-by who approached, then picked up her shopping bags and drove home. It was only when the pain did not subside that she discovered her arm was broken. Her stoicism was remarkable, but it did not always serve her well: it took her far too long to receive her cancer diagnosis, as she ignored the first symptoms.

Still, she accepted whatever came her way. She did not question when something bad happened, just looked to improve it. And if she could not do that, she soldiered on. Pain had not damaged her; it had somehow opened her up to feel more, understand better. She seemed enviably resilient in life, not only moving forward but doing so in her energetic, forceful, dynamic way.

After her diagnosis in 2015, as her illness progressed she was no longer able to sit for long periods at the dining table, and her appetite became increasingly small. Sometimes it was hard to watch. One day, after seeing that the effects of her sickness were more pronounced, I called her on the phone, sobbing, telling her I did not know how I would cope without her. She was the person I called every morning after I dropped my children to school, and she was a fixture in so many parts of my life. I knew that my crying pained her, but I think she was also comforted to know how much she meant to me, to all of us. 'Darling Rach-ell-e,' she said, pronouncing the 'ch' in my name with a guttural Germanic emphasis. 'Everything must come to an end. But that does not mean that it is the end of all things. I will be gone from here one day, but I will always be with you.'

I no longer had to be convinced to believe in the same things she did. I knew what she had told me was true.

Thirty-eight

When Mira got sick, her children sprang into action. Fred, Jeannette and I joined her at each of her doctor's appointments, where Mira could often be counted upon to deliver a bon mot about her condition. Lilianne would call daily for updates. We did not know exactly how long Mira had left to live, but we tried to stretch the moments out. For my birthday in August 2016, I threw an elaborate family dinner party at my home. I was turning fifty, but it was a grand farewell to my mother as much as anything else. Pink roses in silver vases lined the table, and everyone wore sparkly party hats. When I gave a speech, I touched softly on the love we all felt for her, hoping she would later hold my words close to her heart.

I tried to repeat the festive atmosphere at a Sunday lunch four months later, when Lilianne had flown in from the US. I had asked my friend and neighbour Mirko, who occasionally sang professionally, to serenade Mira with an Italian song in his hypnotic baritone. His agreeing to do so reminded me how moments of kindness can be so affecting. By then, Mira had deteriorated considerably, and almost bowed out that day, having woken up feeling dizzy and nauseous. But when she eventually arrived she felt better, and closed her eyes while she concentrated on Mirko's voice. I, too, kept my eyes shut, not just to stop the tears from collecting but also to glean the joy from the moment, rather than the sorrow.

Before Mira had grown so ill, her Australia-residing children felt like we were members of a secret society: we started to develop a shorthand between us, speaking several times a day to compare intelligence on our mother's state. In Mira's final six months, Lilianne flew over twice – moving in with her and helping with her home care – and it must have been difficult feeling like an outsider to our newly formed clan. Our approaches in handling our mother's illness differed, and there were times when it was fraught.

There were days and nights when I looked after my mother and felt panicky: once, in the middle of the night, she woke up in terrible pain and I was helpless, having already administered her full dose of medicine. I called the hospital's palliative care unit and spoke to the nurse in charge, pleading for direction. Those minutes of watching my mother groan, before I found out what I should do, seemed like failure.

At the same time, I was often aware of the honour bestowed on me: my mother had nursed and fed me when I was a baby, wiping my brow when I was sick, changing my clothes when they were soiled. It is such a momentous task to mother someone, and I felt the circularity of that gift when I was able to return it to Mira. My mother, who had never liked to ask for help, was now relying on all of her children to do every small task. We had the responsibility of that, and one greater: it was her fervent wish to die at home, and we promised we would allow that to happen.

We tried to keep up with the escalating changes of her illness. A rotation of nurses began to arrive, both to ease the load and perform some of the tasks we could not do alone. Among them, we had our favourites, and began to discern which ones would chatter incessantly and who did their job in silence. Mira usually preferred the latter. We labelled Mira's kitchen drawers with coloured stickers indicating whether the dishware inside was to be used for *fleishig* (meat) or *milchig* (milk) meals, since the nursing staff were not always familiar with the laws of *kashrut*, keeping kosher. We all tried to coax our mother with her favourite foods, but watched her shrink instead, save for her stomach, which became more swollen as her tumour grew. She no longer looked like herself; a greyish pallor replaced her light olive complexion and her hazel eyes began to lose their light.

My son, Julian, came to sing his bar mitzvah *parsha* for her, knowing that she would not be alive by the time he turned thirteen that September. He had been sitting in classes with a rabbi for the past six months, a detailed exercise in which he had to learn how to pronounce the Hebrew words and apply the correct melody to each chant. His bar mitzvah would land on Shabbat Shuva, also known as the Shabbat of Return – the special period of repentance between the Jewish New Year and Day of Atonement. The portion my son sang centred on God's kindness in forgiving His people. Julian's voice was still high and crisp, and it rang out proudly and strongly in my mother's lounge room. When he stood in front of her recliner and recited the prayers, I had to turn away so neither he nor my mother could see the tears flooding my eyes.

Later that week, I asked her to sit outside and say a few words that I could film and later play when Julian's big day of bar mitzvah celebration arrived. Of course, she had nothing rehearsed and no longer sounded like herself; her voice had dulled, and her speech was slower. But her message, as always, remained clear and sound. And she started with a question that reminded me of the old Mira: 'How do I look?'

As she spoke, I was reminded of several things. Even in the depth of her illness, she could still speak off the cuff, her words never getting jumbled. This, despite the fact that English was not her native language, was remarkable to me. Understandably, her words were more melancholy than usual. She began:

'To my darling Julian: I loved you from the minute you were born, and your grandfather Manny had exactly the same feeling. Maybe you remember the game you played with him: pushing Zaida's hat off his head while he was sitting in his chair, and you would be laughing, and Zaida would be laughing too.

'There are a lot of snippets of memories that I would like to bring forward so that they stay with you when you are older. First of all, you were always a very, very good child, and a very good grandchild. And you loved everyone. I couldn't forget how helpful and loving you were – and still are, of course. And I love you every, every day more and more.

'I am trying to enjoy the rest of the time that I have to see you as much as I can, and to love you as much as it's possible. I wish you a very, very nice bar mitzvah, my darling. You deserve the best of everything because you give a lot of yourself. Whenever you come see me, you always give me the most heartfelt hugs, and you tell me, "Nana, you are the best nana." I do appreciate it very, very much, even though I don't know why I would deserve it. I cannot do much for you now – I can't play, I can't tell stories, I cannot do anything. I just sit in the chair. But you somehow feel that it is a nice and close relationship we have. You are a wonderful person and you will be a beautiful grown-up, and you can achieve anything you want. Stay on the Jewish path. Be good to your mother and father and sister. I love you, my darling. God bless you.'

* * *

Not long after that, my mother worsened. At one point she slipped into a state of unconsciousness, and the doctors were not sure she would wake again. But she did, and although she was hardly eating and barely said a word, there was a remarkable lifting of her spirits when Rabbi Shmuel Karnowsky, then the rabbi at Elwood synagogue, paid a visit. We sat with my mother – her four children encircling her – and the rabbi led us in uplifting song. '*Avinu Malkeinu, Choneinu V'aneinu, ki ein banu ma'asim.*' These words are asking God to answer our prayers, and to deal kindly and gently with us. It is a song that asks for salvation. That was a moment of overwhelming beauty shared between all of us, a collective goodbye. It was like a snapshot of my mother's life: both achingly sad and terribly beautiful, so beautiful and sad together that sometimes you can barely stand to look at it.

* * *

There were false alarms for two days. Together with my siblings, I stayed with Mira for long stretches, leaving only to put my children to bed. One night, Jeannette fell asleep holding her hand, remaining that way for hours. Our mother lay in a rented hospital bed in her lounge room, since her own bed had become too uncomfortable for her to lie in. The lounge was the room with the most light in the house, and sun would stream through the gauzy curtains during the day. We tried to remove any of the sterility that the bed brought with it, covering its ugly brown baseboard with photos of some of Mira's grandchildren and great-grandchildren. But it was hard to cheer up the room. It held too much waiting, too much heaviness.

Mira no longer opened her eyes, and it was difficult to tell if she knew what was going on. Once, when I was alone with her, I kneeled by her side and whispered in her ear: 'Make sure you visit me after you're gone.' In that moment, I faltered slightly: wouldn't it be better if we agreed on a symbol, a sign she could use to let me know she was still with me, even after she had left the earth? I looked around the room, my eyes settling on one of the ornaments on her mantel. I chose that. And then I added quietly, 'If you want to be with your *Mamush* again, you should go. She will be waiting for you.'

It was late at night and I was at home when one of my siblings called and told me to come quickly. Julian and Zoë were both half-asleep when I ushered them to the car. Jeannette and Lilianne were already at Mira's, and Fred was also en route. While I drove, my sisters put me on speakerphone, so that Mira could hear me too in her final moments. Her breathing had changed, they said, and the end was very close. From the car, I joined them in song – we all sang the sacred prayer *Adon Olam*, struggling with the final lyrics, our voices cracking, our words becoming incoherent: '*Adonai li v'lo ira.*' God is with me; I shall not fear. We tried to usher my mother out with the voices she had loved so fiercely.

Once I arrived, I bolted up the stairs. Everyone was teary, and I could not tell if I had missed her death. But I thought there was a chance that she was still close, that she had a few seconds to hear me even though her heart had stopped. What was there to say? 'I love you, I love you. Thank you. You gave me everything.'

* * *

In accordance with Jewish practice, someone had to stay in the room with my mother: the *shomer*, the watcher, the guardian of the dead. I had deposited my children downstairs, and it was there that I went to break the news of their grandmother's death. My ten-year-old daughter was puzzled. 'Didn't you say that after Nana's mother died, she sent her signs? Can you ask Nana to send us a sign now?' I tried to explain that it did not quite work that way, that signs did not arrive because you had asked for them; they floated in of their own accord when you needed them most. 'I do need a sign,' Zoë insisted. 'Can you go back and ask Nana for one, please?'

I was not quite sure what to do, and I felt sad, and foolish, as I entered the room again. But I also felt compelled to fulfil my daughter's request. When I walked to my mother's side, I did not feel that death had taken over the room just yet. I knew Mira was no longer alive, but I sat next to her anyway, and spoke almost apologetically. 'Mum, Zoë says she would like a sign.' It felt ridiculous, and I already tried to imagine what I would say to Zoë when I returned to her. But here is the thing: as soon as those words left my lips, one of the photos taped to Mira's baseboard suddenly slipped and swung on its side. All the other photos remained in place. The photo in question? A smiling portrait of my children: Zoë in braids, leaning into Julian's shoulder. I went to tell Zoë that her Nana had not changed, even in death. She always delivered what you asked for.

* * *

The next day, Mira's four children met at the *Chevra Kadisha*, the burial house that oversees all matters relating to a Jewish funeral. We went through the paperwork, confirming biographical details about our mother, agreeing on the time for the funeral. In Jewish law, the burial happens quickly, based on a biblical command: 'Thou shalt surely bury him the same day.' It is considered unseemly to leave the body on earth with the living when the person's soul has already returned to God. We settled on the next day at midday, giving family members time to fly in from interstate and overseas. In line with the rituals of shiva, the seven-day mourning period, we were each given low, black chairs to sit on – the uncomfortable seats which act as a constant reminder that one is grieving. We were informed that the clothes we wore to the funeral would be ripped, as Jewish law prescribes. At the cemetery, we would take it in turns to cut each other's lapels, right over our hearts, the tearing of our garments acting as a physical embodiment of our sorrow.

The weather had been glorious all week, and so it continued on that early April day. I was driving Lilianne, and a minute after we pulled away from the *Chevra Kadisha* and stopped at a red light, a white bird – its belly bluish-grey – landed on the centre of my car's windscreen, its wings outstretched, and tapped it gently. It wasn't like I had run into the bird; it seemed to have chosen that spot deliberately and only momentarily. Lilianne screamed. 'Oh my God, what the hell was that? That was the weirdest thing!'

It took me a while to collect myself and tell her: before she died, when I asked Mira to visit me, I had looked around her living room and spied a blue porcelain bird on her mantelpiece. 'Let's make it a blue bird,' I had said to her, thinking that butterflies were too clichéd.

Another strange thing; another moment for pause.

* * *

Jewish funerals are stark and shocking: given their proximity to the time of death, it is hard for anyone to act contained. They are brutal in many ways: after the mourners' clothes are ripped and eulogies are given, everyone gathers at the gravesite, a deep hole in the ground. Mira's plot was next to Manny's, and we all stood there while the casket dropped into the ground with a loud thud, the kind of noise that hurts your body when you hear it.

Before the rabbi could recite the burial Kaddish, we were instructed to fill the grave with the surrounding earth. There were shovels placed in the soil for us to do so – custom forbids the shovel to be passed directly from hand to hand, so that the tragedy of death does not spread – and we each took turns to throw earth on Mira's final resting place. Soon, other mourners stepped in to help; shovelling the earth is an honoured role fulfilled by close family, friends and those willing to share the burden of the task.

After the service, we washed our hands, adhering to the custom of purification. It would be almost a year before we returned to the cemetery for the consecration, the unveiling of the tombstone. Each of Mira's children had contributed to the words that appeared, but I remember how adamant I was that the language relating to the Holocaust was clear and without euphemisms. And so the inscription included:

She witnessed her father murdered by the Nazis/Her mother, brother and sister were killed in the Holocaust/She survived four concentration camps/yet still she lived her life with an unwaveringly positive attitude.

Also on her gravestone, the final words she heard from us: *Adonai li v'lo ira.* God is with me; I shall not fear.

Thirty-nine

In the days after my mother's death, an Israeli cousin remarked on how hard that particular loss is. '*Imma zeh imma,*' she said. Mother is mother. I kept returning to these words, and their simple accuracy.

Jewish people don't send flowers when a death occurs; they show up during the shiva period with round-shaped foods such as bagels and eggs, symbolising life and renewal. But more significantly, they come to tell stories about the deceased and exchange memories they possess, and it is then that you realise fully the impact that someone has had. A neighbour from across the road, a stranger to us, slipped a handwritten letter under Mira's door. She knew that Mira was a Holocaust survivor, she wrote, and would see her from a distance – longing to approach her, but feeling too shy, even though my mother would smile at her when their paths crossed on the street. 'I wanted to express to you my sorrow at her death, and my regret that I never did work up the nerve to go and knock on her door,' she wrote. 'I am no mystic, but

I felt a special energy, some sort of magic, emanating from her home.'

Such was Mira's power.

* * *

For the second Shabbat evening following Mira's death, her family decided to share the meal in her home. There was something stabilising about the consistency of her place, which had been unchanged for many years. We dressed the table the same as always: the white tablecloth with its floral cutwork, the silver candlesticks, the sweet challah bread dotted with sesame seeds. We even tried to re-create her actual dishes: her sauerkraut soup, with its touch of vinegar; her sour-bitter lettuce dressing that balanced oil, lemon and salt in careful quantities; her poppyseed cake, with its secret ingredient of lemon zest, moist and slightly tangy and covered in a glaze of shiny bittersweet chocolate. Between courses, I stole down to her bedroom, inhaling the scent of her scarves so I could conjure her up once more. It did not feel sad; it felt comforting.

All night, Jeannette was in a mild frenzy; when she arrived at the house, an alert on her car informed her that her keys could not be detected. The employees at the car dealership claimed that was impossible: if she had left her keys somewhere else, the car's engine would have cut out after a few blocks. As it was, she had driven from her work.

We searched through every pocket in her bag, every inch of her car, uncovering a lost pair of sunglasses that she had not seen in two years. Still, no keys. Road assistance was called, and a tall, calm mechanic with the air of a gentle sage turned up. When we asked whether she could have driven her car all the way from work without its key, he had a strange response. 'Ghosts are real,' he said.

'Excuse me?' I was not sure I had heard him correctly.

He said it once more. 'Ghosts are real.' He said it slowly this time, as if Jeannette and I had limited understanding of spirits as well as cars.

'It's interesting you should say that,' said Jeannette, 'because our mother passed away two weeks ago.'

The man nodded. 'You must pray to your mother to find the keys,' he told her. And then he left.

In the end, Jeannette called a taxi to take her home. On the way, she stopped at her office, wanting to check her car spot there. It was empty. For some reason, she asked the cab driver to wait while she walked fifteen metres up the road. A glistening object on a speed hump caught her eye. Moonlight? No. The keys, of course. She never could work out how that had happened.

* * *

I was never a regular synagogue-goer until my mother died. But when I felt overwhelmed by a barrage of feelings – grief, loss, fear – I needed to pour them somewhere outside of myself. I was a member of St Kilda synagogue, housed in a historic building with a sweeping domed ceiling. There was a male choir, and their operatic voices would lift me; after the stirring *Adon Olam* was completed – the service's final, joyous song – I would always need to dab my eyes with a tissue. I had not yet found a way to replace the daily communications

I'd shared with Mira; I did not try to talk to her aloud and pretend she was on the other end of a telephone line. But the way my wounds seemed to fill a little with each chorus sung in the synagogue, and the way I felt a modicum of ease by the time I exited, made me feel like I had found another way to connect with her. I already believed in God; that was nothing new. But now, more than ever, I believed in the strength of a mother's love.

* * *

For three years I found myself in a grief chamber, not knowing how to get out. Early on I explained grief to a friend like this: You know you're about to go on a journey to a rather bleak and desolate part of the world. You've travelled to a nearby region previously, so you think you're prepared. You've packed a suitcase, you've read the travel guides. But when you arrive, it's not at all like you expected. You weren't counting on the atmosphere in this country, which is unlike any you've been to before. It's like stepping into a grey bubble, where the air is so constricted that it affects everything else. It's like you packed the wrong clothes, read the wrong guides. You can't even breathe properly there, and no one warned you about that part at all.

In Jewish law, you mourn a parent for the duration of a year. It is longer than one mourns a spouse, where the grieving period is halved, mainly because the laws have a practical application. After the twelve months had elapsed, I thought I had adjusted to a parentless life. I holidayed with my children, I immersed myself in work. I ignored the signals my body was sending to put me on alert. I felt sluggish; I could not concentrate. One day, I went to the salon and asked for my hair to be cut into a fringe. It exposed a section of my scalp that I had never seen before. 'Why is it like this?' I asked my hairdresser. 'You're losing hair,' he said. In high school, I was known for my mass of curls, which heralded my arrival before friends could make out my face, so thick that I could barely put it into a ponytail without breaking several elastic bands. It was not like that anymore.

I continued this way for several periods of Yizkor, the anniversary of Mira's death. At the three-year mark, St Kilda *shule*'s Rabbi Glasman called to wish me 'long life' – the customary condolence, which continues the theme that Judaism focuses on living rather than death. He told me something I had not realised: the reason there is a prescribed twelve-month mourning period for one's parents – incorporating strict regulations, such as not attending any parties – is so that when that time has come to an end, the mourner knows that they have grieved properly and should not feel guilty about living their life fully again. I had held on to my sadness as a way of holding on to my mother, as if it were a symbol I could show the world, an expression of my love for her that linked us still. But by holding on to my grief for so much longer than twelve months, I was in direct opposition to what my religion asked of me.

He also explained the other phrase so commonly uttered at the time of someone's death: 'May their memory be a blessing.' It is an instruction of sorts. The proper way to honour a loved one is to continue their goodness in life, because they are unable to do so themselves. It is a blueprint for moving forward: it shows that there is a way a person can continue to live on earth long after they have left it. They do so through the good deeds and honourable acts performed in their name. It was something I could do; something I *would* do.

* * *

I don't think my mother believed that a 'lasting love' was the only way to find happiness. Happiness did not arrive on your doorstep through another person; it was a choice that you needed to make all the time. Happiness is in living now so that you don't regret anything later. Happiness is there for the taking, although sometimes you have to reach out far to grab it.

Having not reached for it for so long, I was not sure I even knew how to do so. But, determined to let my grief go, I began to allow slices of light into my days: noticing when fallen flowers beautified the pavement on my walks; petting the soft ears of panting dogs when they passed me; marvelling when I read something so beautifully precise that I would weep.

I thought about my mother's words in the card she had written me. For a long time, I believed only in the possibility of darkness: accidents happen, illnesses occur, my mother would die, my life would be empty without her. Yet perhaps my mother's words were not a prediction, but a fact: The Happiness Is Near because the happiness is always near. You have to believe in it.

And then, a little more than three years after Mira died, I met a man and fell in love. Our romance began slowly: first, a friendship formed, and we took many long walks together. It only occurred to us later that there was more than friendship there. My parents would have liked him very much: his keen intelligence, his gentle manner, his tenderness towards me. I thought of how my mother would have reacted to him: his twinkling eyes might have reminded her of Yanchi, the brother she adored and lost. She would have recognised more similarities: a warm smile, humour, kindness.

It saddened me that she never got to meet him, until I realised one day that she had. He and I had gone to the same high school, and when I was fifteen and he eighteen, he had asked me on a double date. I thought him handsome and smart, but I wasn't sure what he thought of me; there never was a second date. Neither of us can remember why.

But I know that he must have come to my house to pick me up – my parents were traditional in that respect – and Mira would have made sure to meet him first, before allowing me to go with him. The thought of this scene brings me solace; I did not know then that he was my *beshert*, my destiny, but I like to imagine that a part of her did.

Sometimes, at night, I lie in bed and try to summon Mira, the way she did with Genya. I close my eyes tightly, and I remember the smell of her hairspray, the softness of her skin. I can hear the lilting sound of her voice, the caress of her well-chosen words. And sometimes, when I whisper into the night and tell her about my love, I feel my mother's happiness land gently on my heart.

* * *

Before she died, I looked up what my mother's name meant. It is a name that is common in many languages, but means different things in each: peace (Russian), wonderful (Latin), ocean (Sanskrit), goodness/kindness (Albanian), abundance (Greek). It is a name infused with all these favourable words, until you get to Hebrew. In Hebrew, Mira means bitter.

When Mira was reminded of this, she was amused. I was indignant, thinking that she deserved a better name. It was only later that I investigated the role that bitterness plays in Judaism. One of the key ingredients at the Seder table for the Passover holiday is bitter herbs, or *maror*. At that Seder meal, the *maror* – which is usually something like romaine lettuce or horseradish – is eaten together with charoset: a sweet apple, nut, cinnamon and sugar mixture. We do this because we acknowledge the hardship that the Jewish people have experienced in the past, and we understand that life incorporates the bitter and the sweet as side-by-side companions.

I did not know anyone whose life incorporated these two pillars to the extent that my mother's did. But she did not let bitterness overwhelm her life. She had seen the worst of humanity, yet she chose to concentrate on the best of it. She had seen life expunged as if it were meaningless, yet she chose to invest her own life with purpose. She had been close to death, yet she had decided to live. There is only one way to describe it. And it is long after her death that I realise that 'Mira' forms the start of that word: Miracle.

It turns out there was no more fitting name for my mother.

* * *

What was the point of my mother's suffering? Did it mean anything in a wider sense? Was there some kind of design?

I've never found an adequate reason to explain the tragedy that befell her. But like Mira, I have learned that not every question needs an answer and not every problem has a solution.

For instance, I sometimes ask myself whether the hatred my mother experienced could happen in my lifetime. It is a question about possibility, and I've learned that many things are possible. Love, yes, but also hate and cruelty. Yet I do imagine that there is a counterpoint to that: to act with kindness and goodness. And, perhaps, to have faith in something greater, something unexplainable, that carries beyond what we know and allows us to stretch our minds further. I do not know what lies ahead, and I cannot understand all that has passed.

I think about a psalm that is recited at many Jewish and non-Jewish funerals alike, with the words 'Man is like a breath, his days are like a passing shadow.' If one believes that life on earth is just a precursor for the days to come, it is not for us to dissect everything that has taken place and assign logic to each scene that has played out in our life's film. My mother believed. And to carry on all that she taught me, I have to believe as well.

* * *

In 1996, I sent a letter to distinguished author and Nobel Peace Prize winner Elie Wiesel, who wrote of his Holocaust experiences so powerfully and to such acclaim in several books, with *Night* being the one I could never forget. I was living in New York, and felt compelled to tell him a little of my mother's story, and express how reading his book had allowed me to better understand what she had been through.

A few weeks later, I received a response from him in the mail, handwritten on Boston University letterhead, where he was a professor.

June 23, 1996
Dear Rachelle Unreich —
Simply: thank you for your warm and moving letter —
I wish you well.
Please convey my greetings to your mother.
— Elie Wiesel.

I have held that letter close for all these years. Not only for what his writing had meant to me, and for the graciousness he had shown by responding this way, but also because it was a talisman of sorts: one day, I would write my mother's story, too.

Epilogue

It has been six years since Mira died. My son Julian is now nineteen, and my daughter Zoë is almost seventeen, the same age at which her grandmother Mira was taken from her home in Spišská Stará Ves to the first concentration camp. She reminds me of my mother in some ways: she wakes up singing, as she has done ever since she was a toddler, and I can often hear her tuneful voice threading through the corners of our home. It makes me wonder the extent to which features and temperament get passed down from generation to generation. I wonder how much of Mira is in me.

Did her trauma leave an imprint on me, in my genes? I grew up without any grandparents and – because of the Holocaust – none of my surviving aunts and uncles lived in the same country as me. There was only a lone first cousin, a generation older than me, who lived in Melbourne. Yet I did not feel unlucky or deprived. I had two parents who believed I could do anything, who saw unlimited potential in me, who treasured and cherished me.

I miss Mira deeply, but I feel her absence less. Her heart is embedded in my daughter's kindness, my son's sensitivity. My brother, Fred, will reliably answer the phone when I need to solve a problem; my sister Jeannette will talk to me late at night. Overseas, Lilianne will pepper a conversation with her staccato laughter, so similar to Mira's, and in video calls I see in her my mother's dimples, her fine features. I no longer remember Mira as slack-jawed, grey, ill. Thanks to her stories, I see her in different forms: sometimes as the very young girl with her hair cut into a blunt fringe, standing at the centre front of her class photograph, grinning with all her teeth and happiness showing at once. Sometimes she is the mother of my youth, soft-fleshed and warm. Always she is inextricably Mira: bright-eyed and smiling.

* * *

Lately I have been reminded of the need to hold on to life in all its brilliance. Just over five years after he sang so beautifully to my mother in her final months, my friend Mirko died of an aggressive brain tumour. I wondered if it had already been burrowed into some part of his skull when he appeared at my house that Sunday, performing 'Ti Voglio Tanto Bene' to fewer than a dozen people in the same way he might have for a crowd of hundreds. Why would something so terrible happen to him, a man whose absence surely makes the world less sweet? I choose to believe that we cannot comprehend the reason from our vantage point. But I think of the English translation of the words Mirko sang: 'Tell me that your love will never die/ And like the golden sun/ Will never die.'

And although I have not yet learned how to make sense of the shadowy side of life – the part that is random and unfair and sometimes inexplicably cruel – I now carry a sentiment that my beloved often expresses: 'Tomorrow holds the possibility of being better than today.' The present may appear bleak, and there is no guarantee that tomorrow will be any brighter. But no matter what eventuates, the future always contains that chance for improvement. It was a sentiment my mother lived by, and it is the core of what lies in my heart whenever I commune with God. I do not pray for an outcome. I pray because I believe. For me, faith is not about blind hope; it is not about making wishes and wanting them granted. It is about believing that there is something bigger in the universe than myself.

* * *

I wrote this book during a time when the world was shuttered by a pandemic. I had already endured eighteen months of on-and-off-again lockdowns, and I let most of those monotonous days skip by me while I did what everyone around me was doing: walking, worrying, cooking. Every now and then, I would sit at my computer, trying to put down my thoughts about Mira. After I would print out the resultant pages – only a small handful – I'd draw a big red diagonal line through them. I could not find a way into her story.

One September morning, I went for a walk with my neighbour Diana, Mirko's wife. On the very first day of Melbourne's stringent lockdowns, Mirko was felled by a punishing headache that would not cease. Even though we had all been ordered to stay indoors, here was an exception to the rule: a medical emergency. Diana drove him straight to the emergency room of the local hospital. Soon, a pronouncement: Mirko had a glioblastoma. The couple refused to speculate on any kind of prognosis. They would just take each day as it came. There were always miracles. Medical advances. Something.

Whenever Diana and I took one of our regular walks together, I was aware of two recurring themes in our conversation. She always wanted to hear stories about my mother, and of how her traumatic past had not stopped her from moving forward – from thriving, even. But she was also drawn to the mystical parts of Mira's story, because she found comfort there.

On this particular day, I had been complaining about my career and the decline of print journalism. As an aside, I mentioned Mira: I wanted to ensure her story did not wither away with all the other important histories that disappear. We were mid-step when Diana stopped, turning to face me. 'But isn't writing about your mother your legacy? Isn't that what you truly want to leave behind?'

The word 'legacy' ricocheted across the pavement. It sounds different when it is coming from someone who is living daily with the spectre of death, who has such immediate evidence of life's finality. It stayed with me all through that walk, and I could not get it out of my head thereafter.

The next day, a Saturday, I got up early to sit at my desk. I started writing about Mira, and continued to write furiously day after day, only leaving my post for quick meals, staying in my chair each day until midnight. At the end of six weeks, I had completed my first draft.

* * *

During that period, some weird things. The first: when I write about Olga, Mira's sister, my body begins to shake. Growing up, I had not felt connected to her. But when I learn more about her, when I start studying photos of her – as a bride she looked particularly young and fragile, set off by her gown's Peter Pan collar – I feel the impact of her loss. A weight falls on me, on my body, behind my eyes. The days that I am filling her out on the page, I cannot stop crying. Of course I am sad because her story is tragic. But there is something else. I can't shake the feeling that I am crying Mira's tears.

When it comes to recounting Mira hiding in the barn and needing to move because her allergy to the hay had become so severe, I begin sneezing. It is the beginning of spring, so I put it down to hay fever; I am a sufferer, after all. In years past, I have endured desensitisation injections in the hope that my eyes will be less watery, my nose less runny. Still, I have not had severe hay fever for several years, and this day – when I first write about Mira's hiding spot – is the first time this season that I feel overcome with allergy.

I am dreading writing about my grandfather Dolfie, and when I have finished describing his body lying dead at the front of his house, I need a break. I opt for a coffee from the local cafe at the end of my street, walking around the block as I sip it. When I come back ten minutes later, a confronting sight lies on the pathway leading to my front door: a dead rat, which is being picked over by three black crows. The scene is so bizarre, and also intuitively feels symbolic, leading me to wonder what crows represented in the depiction of Nazi

Germany. I learn that when German troops first descended on Prague in 1939, Czech radio broadcaster Franta Kocourek said: 'From somewhere far away, a huge, black crow has flown into Prague.'

One last thing, as I was nearing the end of Mira's time in concentration camps. I listen to her recorded voice, and hear her terror when she talks about the German shepherd that was often set upon the prisoners in Neustadt-Glewe during the brutal roll call. That day, I go to do something in my backyard, but just as I turn the handle of my back door, a dog leaps at the flywire screen, barking wildly. I am shocked and confused; I do not have a dog, and my yard is fenced off. It turns out that my gardener has brought his rescue dog over, having never done so before, and it has momentarily escaped from his grip, frightened by the unexpected noise I made.

Not for the first time, I feel like I have found a portal into my mother's story. Somehow, I am not merely retelling it. A fraction of it is being revealed to me, in the tiniest of ways. I try not to ascribe any further meaning to it, but just accept it as it happens. When my heart starts racing as I write about my mother in hiding, so often on the verge of being caught, it makes sense to me. Perhaps our mother–daughter roles have finally flipped, and just as she felt the pain and pleasure of my every setback and achievement when I was growing up, I now have a visceral experience of her story, too.

* * *

People will often instruct someone to put the past behind them: to move forward, to get on with it, to close a chapter. But for me, travelling backwards in time has been at once painful and rewarding, both sobering and uplifting. Although it has been the source of secrets and mysteries, I have learned that I cannot otherwise fill in the gaps that lie within. Returning to the past has made me whole, or at least closer to whole than I was before.

We have not sold our mother's home, and nearly seven years later we still meet there occasionally for Shabbat dinners, keeping our memories locked in a time capsule of sorts. Some people don't understand it; they can't see why we would return to her house again and again, to sit at a table laden with the past. Everything is imbued with a memory of her: when I am in her kitchen, I remember her shelling walnuts and grating apple to make charoset for our Seder meal at Passover. When I see the boxy air-conditioning unit, I think of her sitting in front of it during the summer months, trying to cool herself when the sweatiness of her illness made her overheat. It was when she was in that position that I tried to bring in a meditation teacher, who gave her a mantra she could recite when she needed to relax. She listened to him kindly, and afterwards he thanked me profusely for bringing him there, asking for no money for his efforts. She never used the skills he taught her; she had her own mantra. Family. Love. Faith.

It is not so much about preserving the past, but incorporating it into the present, like carrying a favourite embroidered handkerchief in the pocket of a coat. It is in the house that our family's collective story lies: not only in the piles of paraphernalia that my mother collected and kept (from my 1981 school report, in which the geography teacher wrote: 'Rachelle made no real effort this term'), but in the way the house makes us feel. Sometimes, I will go there so as not to forget the softness of my mother's skin.

Apart from being the custodians of her house, we are the custodians of her story, her history, her place in history. We have taken over the role she once fulfilled. For so long, Mira acted as the *shomer*, the person appointed to guard the dead. It was a job she neither asked for nor wanted. And now we do it in her stead.

Yet this is not the sum total of Mira's story. She was a guardian of the dead, it is true. But equally she knew how to live, and she passed that knowledge on to us: our own inheritance. To spend it properly, we have to love as strongly as she once did, to feel as mightily, to celebrate as joyously, to give as selflessly. Once, people tried to extinguish her very being. They tried to snuff her out, as if she were a candle that one could pinch to stop from burning. And if not her body, then her essence: her light, her *nefesh*, her soul, her spirit.

They did not even come close to doing so.

Sources

There were times when writing this book felt akin to going on an archaeological dig, where I was constantly unearthing pieces of my mother's story to make it whole. My starting point was Mira's first-hand account, and I had plenty of material: I had conducted numerous interviews with her in the months before her death, and she had previously given three recorded testimonies about her devastating experiences during the Holocaust.

To fill in the gaps in the larger sweep of her life, I first reached out to family. My siblings Alfred, Jeannette and Lilianne (Milgrom) generously shared their own memories, thereby trusting me with a story that is as much theirs as mine. Relatives added more material: Heshek's children, Shoshi and Michael Blumenstock, in Israel; and Shani's daughter, Ruth Leibowitz, as well as Mira's cousin Kurt Storch, both in the United States.

Piecing together David Milgrom's escape from Treblinka was less straightforward. Both my mother and her brother

Heshek had recorded their version of Pavel's biography based on what they recalled of his story, and Jeannette once interviewed him in Yiddish, taking notes in English. The results were far from complete. Research led me to a handwritten document in Hebrew at Yad Vashem, the World Holocaust Remembrance Center in Israel, filed under a name that was barely close to Pavel's. When I had it translated, courtesy of Moty Ickowicz, it seemed to match Jeannette's records. That discovery led me to a more comprehensive report at the United States National Archives and Records Administration (NARA). Sometime around August 1943, Pavel had given a testimony, and on 13 January 1944 his account was written up as a thirteen-page letter by American Vice Consul Roy M Melbourne at the US Consulate in Istanbul, Turkey, addressed to the Secretary of State in Washington, USA. This find was extraordinary to me. Pavel had wanted to tell his story and make people listen. His children were able to hear it in full for the first time – they never knew his report existed – and realised the attempts he made to convey it to the world.

Many historians, academics and people working in the field of Holocaust study and remembrance assisted me along the way. I owe an enormous debt to Emeritus Professor Dr Konrad Kwiet, who played such a significant part in my waking thoughts that he occasionally popped up in my dreams, too. As the current Resident Historian at the Sydney Jewish Museum, he helped ensure that my work was factually correct, and did not hesitate to answer my late-night and weekend emails. He discovered – unbeknown to me or Mira during her lifetime – that my mother had been part of a selection at Auschwitz, headed by Josef Mengele. Professor Kwiet has backed me from the start, and it has meant so much to have someone as well-recognised in the field as he is on my side. Through him, doors were opened: he connected me to Distinguished Professor Emeritus Richard Breitman at American University, Washington, DC, who helped me track down the US Consulate document via David Langbart at the National Archives at College Park, Washington, DC, and to Professor Jan Grabowski at the University of Ottawa. Professor Kwiet not only encouraged me in a fulsome way, but remains an inspiration through his dogged and brilliant contributions to Holocaust study. I feel honoured to know him.

So many others aided my research. Jan Láníček, from the University of New South Wales, showed a dedicated interest in my work, and given that he is an expert on the subject of the Holocaust in Czechoslovakia, was a perfect guide. Emeritus Professor Tuvia Friling of Ben-Gurion University of the Negev in Israel steered me on the topic of Istanbul intelligence and the Working Group, while the esteemed Professor Yehuda Bauer – a giant in the field of Holocaust study – responded to my queries about Eliyahu Laufer.

I had great assistance from various Holocaust museums and institutions around the world. On my doorstep is one of the finest, the Melbourne Holocaust Museum. There, CEO Jayne Josem has been so supportive, while co-president Sue Hampel and the Manager of Adult Education and Academic Engagement, Dr Simon Holloway, both looked closely at much of the book, picking up important points.

At Auschwitz-Birkenau Memorial and Museum, director of the Centre of Research, Piotr Setkiewicz PhD, and deputy head Jacek Lachendro PhD, went through the Auschwitz portions of my book and answered endless questions. Their help was invaluable. Likewise, at the KL Plaszow Muzeum in Poland, Kamil Karski answered a flood of my emails with in-depth, thoughtful and speedy responses, going far beyond the call of duty. At the Sered Holocaust Museum in Slovakia, Dr Martin Korčok PhD and his colleague Kristina Svrčková were happy to indulge my desire to know the smallest of details, responding to my queries with consideration and patience.

I had dealings with Yad Vashem, the World Holocaust Remembrance Center in Israel, and the United States Holocaust Memorial Museum (USHMM) in Washington, DC (where I need to single out Bashi Packer), as well as with Łukasz Kukawski at the Sobibor Museum in Poland and the Treblinka Museum. Finally, the Memory of Treblinka Foundation helped me tremendously, and my thanks goes to the chair of the board, Ewa Teleżyńska-Sawicka, board member Paweł Sawicki and also through them: Alina Skibińska; USHMM Poland Representative; and sociologist Dr Karolina Panz, both members of the Polish Centre for Holocaust Research.

Archival material online helped provide answers to research: the Arolsen Archives (International Center on Nazi Persecution), the Joint Australia (National Director Brett Kaye has been of wonderful assistance) and YIVO Institute for Jewish Research. Others who helped are Peter Absolon, who runs the Kosice-based Slovakia Genealogy Services and both Mikulas Liptak and Madeleine Isenberg who co-authored *Jews in the Spis Region, Vol. I, Kežmarok and its Surroundings* (2010, ViViT s.r.o. (Ltd) Kežmarok, Slovakia).

So many were gracious when I approached them: Richard Brownstein, lecturer at Yad Vashem and author of *Holocaust Cinema Complete: A History and Analysis of 400 Films, with a Teaching Guide*; Oleg Beyda, lecturer at the University of Melbourne; author Bram Presser; Dr Dvir Abramovich, Chair of the Anti-Defamation Commission and Israel Kipen Director of Jewish Studies at the University of Melbourne. I am grateful to the descendants of those who lived in Spišská Stará Ves with my mother, who had unbearable stories of their own families. A special thank you to George Kuchel, who allowed me to write about his father, Otto, to whom he attributes 'kindness and decency'. And I need to extend my appreciation to David M Baron, my first cousin once removed in the US, who has written about my father's family in his book, *The Undercover Wrestler: The Untold Story of an Undercover Hero of Israel*.

To ensure that the Judaic content was accurate, I had the guidance of Rabbi Yaakov Glasman of St Kilda Hebrew Congregation, who jokingly became my 'rabbi on call'. He was the President of the Rabbinical Association of Australasia and was happy to offer sound counsel, answering my questions on Judaism and Jewish culture. I also reached out to Rabbi Shmuel Karnowsky, who applied his sharp eye to some elements of the book.

Despite interviewing my mother at the end of her life, I can't imagine what I would have done without the Holocaust testimonies she gave, the longest of which was conducted by author Elliot Perlman, a friend. He recorded her out of his conviction that her existing testimonies needed to be further expanded, and he did so with great diligence and care, over a period of many weeks. I am so glad that Mira's earliest testimonies were conducted by the Melbourne Holocaust Museum, who twice interviewed my mother over several hours. Robbie Simons, Manager of Digital Storytelling, made it easy for me to share excerpts of these with a wider audience. Additionally, my mother herself felt gladdened that both the Melbourne Holocaust Museum and the USC Shoah Foundation (founded by filmmaker Steven Spielberg) made it their mission to collect as many such testimonies as possible.

I am grateful for the contributions of Edit Rose's daughter Dasha Gilden in Sydney and Julius Scholcz's grandson Ladislav Dlugolinský in Spišská Stará Ves. I relied on a document that was written by a contemporary of my mother, Eugen Šoltýs: *Memories of the Jewish Community of Spišská Stará Ves* (1987). *The Escape Artist: The Man Who Broke Out of Auschwitz to Warn the World* by Jonathan Freedland (John Murray, London, 2022) contained information in it about escapees Czesław Mordowicz and Arnošt Rosin that led me to realise they were the men who Dolfie and Mira had met; without his book, I might never have linked the two episodes.

Other books I used for research included *Belzec, Sobibor, Treblinka: The Operation Reinhard Death Camps* by Yitzhak Arad (Indiana University Press, 1999); *The Treblinka Death Camp: History, Biographies, Remembrance* by Chris Webb and Michael Chocolatý (ibidem Press, Stuttgart, 2021); *If This is a Woman* by Sarah Helm (Little, Brown, London, 2015); *999: The Extraordinary Young Women of the First Official Jewish Transport to Auschwitz* by Heather Dune MacAdam (Hodder & Stoughton, London, 2015); *Living Judaism: The Complete Guide to Jewish Belief, Tradition and Practice* by Rabbi Wayne

D Dosick (HarperCollins Religious, New York, 1998); *The Jewish Way in Death and Mourning* by Maurice Lamm (Jonathan David Publishers, New York, 2000); *Pinkas Hakehillot Slovakia*, edited by Yehoshua Robert Buchler and Ruth Shashak (Yad Vashem, Jerusalem, 2003); *Witness: Voices from the Holocaust* edited by Joshua M Greene and Shiva Kumar (The Free Press, New York, 2000); and *Schindler's Ark* by Thomas Keneally (Hodder & Stoughton, Sydney, 1982). I believe the works of Holocaust survivors – particularly *Night* and *The Fifth Son* by Elie Wiesel, *If This Is a Man* and *The Periodic Table* by Primo Levi, *Man's Search for Meaning* by Viktor E Frankl and *This Way for the Gas, Ladies and Gentlemen* by Tadeusz Borowski – which I first read so many years ago, lodged in my brain and heart in formative ways.

I have told segments of my mother's story in print before: in *The Age* and *Sydney Morning Herald* newspapers' *Spectrum*, in the *Australian Financial Review*, in *Harper's Bazaar*, *Elle* and most recently *Good Weekend* magazines. All of those early editors – Shelley Gare, Marina Go, Kellie Hush, Lindy Percival, Lucinda Pitt and Katrina Strickland – helped me realise that different parts of Mira's story needed to be heard. Several paragraphs within this book first emerged as a Reflections piece for *Good Weekend*, the publication of which inspired me further.

When I recalled Mira's interview for the recipe book *Cooking from the Heart: A Journey Through Jewish Food* by Hayley Smorgon and Gaye Weeden (Hardie Grant, Melbourne, 2012), Gaye was kind enough to track down the original transcript by Tali Borowski, used in that section, which is why the copy in my book differs somewhat from the edited version in the cookbook.

With my background in journalism, I did my utmost to fact-check everything. My mother's story is true, but sometimes memory can be fallible: when Mira first sat down to give an official account, it was almost half a century after the war had ended, and some of her testimonies had tiny discrepancies between them – such as referring to people of certain rank by 'major' in one interview and 'commander' in another. Despite this, her story matched historical records and I could verify almost all of it. I generally quoted her verbatim, unless her English resulted in my needing to delete a word for the reader's comprehension. When I could not verify a name's spelling, I spelled it phonetically; in one case, I changed a family's name at their descendants' request.

In the end, I know I have been faithful to the person my mother was, and the story she has consistently told, and I hope that any oversight on my part does not detract from her very important history. I have done my very best to honour her, to honour the six million Jews who were killed in the Holocaust, and to honour those – like Mira – who survived it.

Acknowledgements

Thank you:

Fred, Jeannette and Lilianne – for sharing Pavel's story with me and having faith that I would portray our mother accurately.

Julian – for your incisive feedback and vision;

Zoë – for your cheer and cheerfulness.

Both of you offered such unending support.

David, Philip and family – with endless respect and love.

Tara Wynne, my extraordinary agent at Curtis Brown, who recognised my work immediately, and who folded me into the final months with her mother, Ruth Arpwood; remembering her and all that we shared. Thank you also to Caitlan Cooper-Trent at Curtis Brown.

Vanessa Radnidge, Head of Literary at Hachette Australia – who believes in magic and makes it happen.

Sara Nelson, VP, Executive Editor at HarperCollins US – I am proud to be part of your legacy of ensuring that future generations learn about the Holocaust.

Fiona Henderson at Bold Type Agency – for moving and shaking, always with passion.

Emeritus Professor Dr Konrad Kwiet – for sharing your vast knowledge, encouragement and care – and for your friendship.

The publishing teams whose excellence and professionalism added so much:

At Hachette: My wonderful and skilled editors Jacquie Brown and Ali Lavau; Louise Stark; Fiona Hazard; Alysha Farry; Lillian Kovats; Kate Taperell; Kirstin Corcoran; Emily Lighezzolo; Chris Sims; Kelly Gaudry; Georgina Harrison, and the sales team and all the excellent staff who worked tirelessly behind the scenes.

At HarperCollins US: Edie Astley, Amy Baker, Emi Battaglia, Lisa Erickson, Stacey Fischkelta, Katie Teas, my endless appreciation.

Emily Hart and Rachel Scully – for early and enthusiastic encouragement.

Andrew Lehmann – who, thanks to serendipity, took photos of me and Mira many years ago and generously allowed their inclusion here.

The memories of Mirko Angele and Adam Port – dear friends who sang and danced their way into my sentences.

Adam, Rebecca and Jake Milgrom; Natalie and Joshua Mendelsohn; Bianca and Anton Merbaum, all of whom Nana Minnie loved so much.

And to Andrew Komesaroff – herein lies the limit to my words. It is not nearly enough to thank you – but I do so anyway – for everything.

Rachelle Unreich started her journalism career when she was completing her Arts/Law degrees at Monash University. In addition to studying writing at UCLA, she has lived in New York, Los Angeles, Sydney and Melbourne. She has been a journalist for 38 years, writing cover stories for *The Age*, *Harper's Bazaar*, *marie claire*, *Rolling Stone* and others, and has had regular columns in the *Sydney Morning Herald*, the *Herald Sun* and *Elle* magazine. Her work has appeared extensively in Australia, the US, UK and South-East Asia. She currently lives in Melbourne.